748.5   63829
Sow

   Sowers.
   Stained glass: an
      architectural art.

ROBERT SOWERS   STAINED GLASS

ROBERT SOWERS

STAINED GLASS:
An Architectural Art

UNIVERSE BOOKS, Inc. New York

63829

First Edition published in the United States of America in 1965
by UNIVERSE BOOKS, Inc., 381 Park Avenue South, New York, New York, 10016

Library of Congress Catalog Card Number: 64–22108
Copyright 1965 in Germany by Verlag Ernst Wasmuth, Tübingen

CONTENTS

INTRODUCTION

To most people stained glass is a "lost art," a glorious and mysterious technique of coloring glass that was perfected in the Middle Ages, later lost, and never to this day rediscovered. In the strict technical sense this is not true. As long ago as 1868, Viollet-le-Duc, restoring the French cathedrals, could claim that his workmen had "completed ancient windows with such a perfection of imitation that one cannot distinguish the restorations from the old parts,"[1] and a long subsequent history of faking medieval stained glass attests to the validity of that claim. Yet there is no getting away from the fact that to this day stained glass remains, even for some of our most distinguished artists and architects, a singularly intractable medium. One wonders therefore what is still somehow lost?

The answer is that no one skill or technique is lost but that several things are very much confused: first of all, our awareness of how the colors in stained glass *are affected in their appearance by the kind of light that falls upon them* – this perhaps more than anything else. Unless one can see what the light is doing to a particular window at any given moment, and how, and why; unless he knows how one might alter either the glass or its setting to obtain some other desired effect, he can have only the most naïve sense of the medium.

Secondly, a sense of how art – any art – can be made to function *as an architectural element* without in the process being reduced to insignificant decoration. Lacking this sense, many of our most able and conscientious architects approach the use of art very cautiously or conservatively, or they avoid it altogether. Yet stained glass more than any other art is dependent upon a viable architectural base for its very existence.

Thirdly – since stained glass is not only an architectural art but in large part a church art – a sense of how to deal with religious themes in an age when art is almost totally secular and private in character.

Confronted with so formidable an array of difficulties one might be justified in declaring the art hopelessly lost except for one indisputable fact: an increasing number of our contemporaries are creating stained-glass windows with as much verve as if they had invented the medium for themselves. Ten years ago it was difficult to point to more than a handful of decent contemporary stained-glass windows. Now, it would be a major project to document the notable work that has been done in half a dozen countries.

Left: 1. Bourges Cathedral, Vaulting of the Choir.

Since this book does not attempt to be such a comprehensive survey, I have chosen to omit certain highly publicized works like Assy, Vence, Hem, Coventry, and the latest windows of Chagall in favor of others of equal merit that are more recent, more experimental or simply lesser known; or equally well-known works which, like Ronchamp, Maria Königin and the First Presbyterian Church in Stamford, most effectively illustrate some particular way of using stained glass. Text and illustrations are closely coordinated throughout the book. I have made every effort to select photographs that would emphasize just the particular qualities under discussion. Whenever some point seemed more graphically demonstrable outside the strict limits of the medium of stained glass, I have not hesitated to digress beyond those limits. I have re-used a few indispensable photographs from *The Lost Art*[2], but in every other respect this is a new book with a new theme. If the burden of the earlier book was to show how stained glass had been not so much lost as thrown away in the Renaissance, and to make a case for its revival, that of the present one is to analyze what, as I have since come to believe after ten years of designing stained-glass windows for new buildings, are the basic hindrances to that revival.

To produce a book of this kind would be impossible without the generous assistance of the many artists, photographers, publishers and others upon whom one must depend for essential photographs and information. I am particularly grateful to the stained-glass artists Rowan Le Compte and Robert Pinart, to Georges Mercier and the editors of *Das Münster* and *Art d'Eglise* for the loan of photographs or assistance in tracking them down; to Alfred Lammer for two photographs from his and John Baker's book, *English Stained Glass*, published by Thames and Hudson; to G. E. Kidder Smith for the loan of several photographs from *The New Churches of Europe* even before that book had come off the presses; to *Art in America* and *Craft Horizons*, *Art International*, and the stained-glass firm of Dr. H. Oidtmann for the loan of plates. Photographs not otherwise credited are in most cases my own.

New York City, April 1965   Robert Sowers

PART ONE: THE MEDIUM OF STAINED GLASS

"Thought is crude, material unimaginably subtle."   Aldous Huxley

I THE TEXTURE OF LIGHT

Even though stained glass along with the other non-naturalistic modes of painting has been in a sense rediscovered in the last hundred years, it is still surrounded for detractors and admirers alike by an aura of undecipherability. Thus Bernard Berenson as recently as 1948 wondered "how much art, as distinct from mere craft, there is in our best twelfth- and thirteenth-century stained-glass windows. Their pattern is not easy to decipher, so much is it melted into the colour; and when deciphered how inferior it is in appeal! I have seen windows, not mere fragments, but entire windows, from St. Denis removed from the interior they were intended to transfigure, and I confess that one's enjoyment of them thus isolated was not so different from the Rajah's gloating over handfuls of emeralds, rubies and other precious stones."[3] André Malraux on the other hand calls the stained glass in Chartres "the supreme paintings of the West, before Giotto," yet goes on to say – however metaphorically – that "stained glass has not been rescued from the medley of strapwork in which Our Lady of the Great Window is engulfed."[4]

One reason for this lingering bafflement is, as I have already suggested, a lack of awareness on the part of the viewer as to just what, in, on, and beyond the surface of the glass determines its appearance. Though stained glass is essentially a two-dimensional art form, an art of the picture plane, we always see *through* it to a greater or lesser degree even when we think that we are simply looking *at* it. We see not merely the light that comes through it but light-modulating elements as well. Often the effect of a stained-glass window is so much a product of what is in our line of vision beyond the glass that if we shift our position a mere foot this way or that the whole effect of the window will be different. When Alfred Lammer and John Baker were photographing windows for their very excellent book, *English Stained Glass*, they sometimes found that they had to photograph them at a considerable angle away from the perpendicular with all of the distortion which that entailed in order to bring out qualities simply not visible head on.[5]

To see how important such background elements can be, let us look at a completely transparent stained-glass window which is located at eye level and actually depends for its effect upon the fullest exploitation of its particular background. The example is an extreme one, for there is no leading or other "strapwork" in the window – nothing but pieces of clear

2. Replacing the West Rose Window of Chartres after World War II.

Pages 12 and 13: 3. and 4. Robert Sowers: Garden Door, New York, 1962.

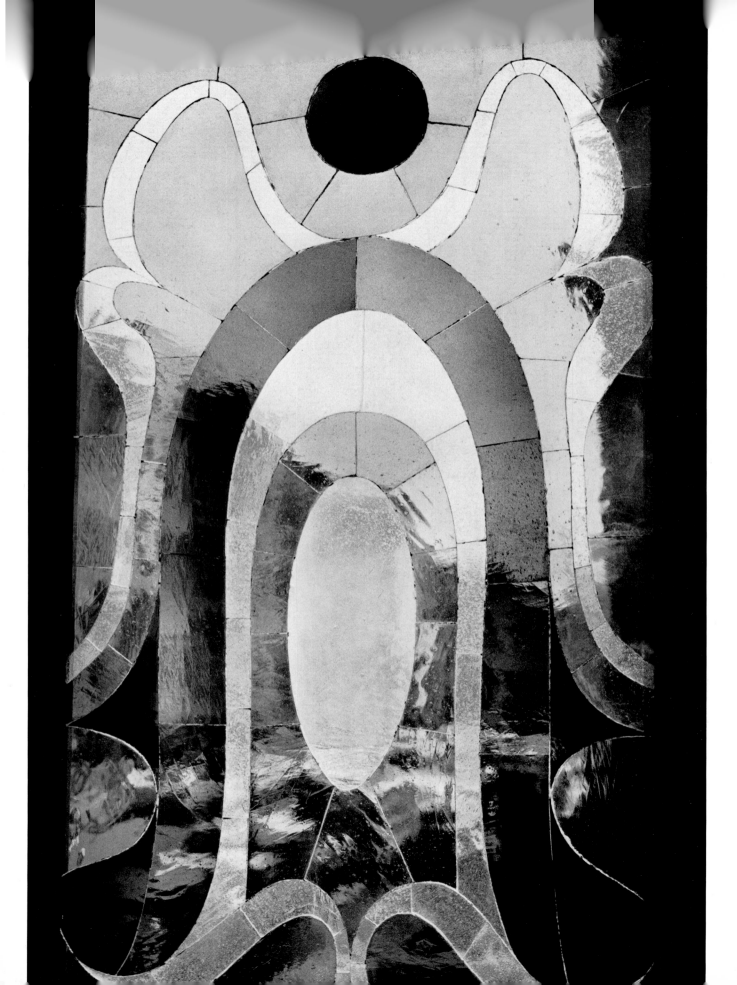

"antique" or handblown glass glued to a sheet of plate glass with transparent epoxy resin. Although such antique glass is absolutely transparent, its surfaces are full of tiny undulations that are a natural product of its viscosity and of the tools with which it is handled while in a molten state. Each such variation or optical imperfection in its surfaces functions like a tiny distorting mirror, picking up and reflecting back to the viewer some random aspect of the field beyond the glass, and it is only when this field includes a range of elements both darker and lighter than the average local tonality of the glass itself that the glass shimmers and sparkles as only stained glass can do. Seen against its intended background of building façades and the like, our example produces an incredibly "glassy" effect. Yet if we view it from near floor level, the upper part, seen against a clear sky, looks as flat and dull as plastic.

This second photograph also enables us to realize what happens to stained glass when it is mounted in light boxes for exhibition. For purely practical reasons of space such installations can seldom be more than a foot deep. Since the inner walls of the box are therefore too close to the focal plane of the glass itself to permit of any variations that would not seem both arbitrary and obtrusive, they must be painted white and evenly illuminated with a diffused light. Seen under such conditions stained glass can only look "flat." All that is left is its color pattern, assuming that the lighting in the installation is adequate and color-corrected, although it is usually neither. In Paris the Chagall windows were beautifully shown, but there the Ministry of Culture built a special pavilion in order to provide them with natural light; the Museum of Modern Art's more typical installation reduced them to little more than life-sized color transparencies of themselves, taken under the least flattering light conditions.

To make our point we chose the extreme example of a totally transparent stained-glass window. It should now be obvious if we examine the surface of a medieval window why the ancient glass that has found its way into museums is less ravaged by such lighting than most contemporary windows. Not only are ancient windows typically much more fragmented with leading and magnificently painted details, but their whole surface is usually covered with a fine patina of scratches and erosion – the dirt of the ages. This seldom shows up in photographs of stained glass but is clearly apparent in the full-size detail on page 35. What such windows have lost in transparency they have gained in a kind of graphic venerability to which we find it hard not to respond; but we must remember that this quality is both foreign to their conception and only by happy accident a quality that makes them relatively exhibition-proof.

It is this quality of the ancient windows that has prevented students of stained glass generally from recognizing how completely whatever is beyond a stained-glass window – eaves, trees, shaded or sunlit walls, or the sky in any of its moods – *becomes an element in the effect of that window.* The more transparent the glass the more prominent such background

Left: 5. "Virgin and St. Anne," Almondbury, Yorkshire, 15th century.
The near transparency of this window is revealed by the protective screening clearly visible through it.

elements become, and the nearer a window is to ground level, the more diverse such elements are likely to be; but even the highest windows in the cathedrals, eroded though they are with age, are still alive to the slightest movement of sun and clouds as anyone who has seen them well knows.

Therefore we must first of all make and keep clear the difference between *transparency* and *translucency*, a difference that is clearly expressed in the words themselves yet often ignored by writers on stained glass who blithely use the words interchangeably: trans*par*ency means literally the passage of appearances through a surface; trans*luc*ency means no less literally the passage of light and light only through a surface. How much depends upon an exploitation of the difference between these two qualities we shall see when we come to discuss the principles of glass painting; but once again: whatever is beyond even the least transparent stained-glass window is always to some degree an element in the effect of that window.

II INSIDE LIGHT VS. OUTSIDE LIGHT

So far we have spoken only about the light that comes through stained glass from light sources outside it. But the effect of that light is very much determined by the amount of light on the viewer's side of the window. When we are indoors, our eyes are adjusted not so much to the full force of daylight as to the light level in our immediate surroundings. In a Romanesque church where the windows are small and widely spaced, the basic light level, even with clear or unglazed windows is quite low. The pupils of our eyes must dilate considerably for us to see anything much at all. Under such conditions the daylight that comes through its windows will appear far, far brighter to us than it ever does out of doors or in a lighter building. In fact, we may establish this rule of thumb that *the apparent brightness of any window opening varies inversely with the light level inside it*. Architecture, in other words, to a large extent determines how luminous a stained-glass window can be. The darker the space (plate 6) the more brilliant will be the light source it creates for stained glass, the lighter the space (plate 7) the more muted that light source will be.

Hence we see why the basic relation between stained glass and its setting has always been dark-to-dark and light-to-light. Given the brilliant, even harsh light of the 12th- and early 13th-century churches, the glassmen very logically composed their windows from a palette of dense, rich colors; or where only white glass could be afforded, they painted the glass with a fine pattern of "grisaille" that breaks up and subdues the light [6] (page 53).

Later, as the walls of the High and Late Gothic churches were opened up to admit more and more light, the point was soon reached where the difference between the outside and inside light level was no longer great enough to fully illuminate the deep ruby-and-blue windows that had been used in the earlier churches. The artists of the 14th and 15th centuries were therefore obliged to work out a viable palette of lighter colors, colors that needed less light to bring them to life, and in the gold and silvery loveliness of the English parish church windows we can see this last major achievement of the medieval glaziers at its best.

In the recent Chapel of the Technical University in Otaniemi, Finland, we see this progression toward lightness pursued to a most charming conclusion. In the back of the chapel is an overhead window that is fifty percent larger than the front window. This raised the interior light level to the point where the architects could place their clear glass wall

Page 18: 6. St. Philibert, Tournus, 11th century. *Photograph: Phélipeaux-Zodiaque.*

Page 19: 7. Sainte-Chapelle, Paris, 1243–48.

8. "La Belle Verrière," Chartres, 12th century; border panels, 13th century.
Right: 9. "The Apostles Window," from Hampton Court, Herefordshire, England,
c. 1435; detail. *Photograph: Courtesy Museum of Fine Arts, Boston.*

10. and 11. Chapel of the Technical University, Otaniemi, Finland; Kaija and Heikki Siren, architects; Rear Window (above) and Altar End (below).

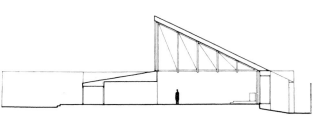

behind the altar without fear of creating any glare in the eyes of the worshipers and could have the magnificent stand of evergreen trees on the site as a lovely natural reredos.

The exceptional instances in which medieval glassmen failed to relate their windows to the prevailing light conditions are as instructive as their generally impeccable practice. The interior of Sainte Chapelle, for example, was actually much too light for the glass of its time, the mid-13th century. Very often therefore, on a sunny day, the light coming through the south windows is bright enough to destroy the effect of the windows

12. Excessive backlighting on a 13th-century window in Canterbury.

13. Gyorgy Kepes: "Light Mural," KLM Royal Dutch Airlines ticket office, New York.

on the north side of the chapel. As this backlight on the north windows increases, the normally rich rubies and blues in them lose all their fire; as the light picks up the bloom of dust and erosion on the inside of the glass, the already dulled colors take on a grayish pallor and all of the bars and armatures and painted areas that function so admirably in silhouette are thrown into unpleasant and busy relief. It is hard for the inexperienced viewer to realize that these windows have not somehow faded.

In Chartres one can see an instance of the opposite failing, a group of windows that are too light for their setting. In 1417, the Vendôme Chapel was built in the south aisle of the nave and glazed with windows that, typical of the later period, are considerably lighter than the original windows of the cathedral. Not only are the aisles of Chartres extremely dark; south windows are generally exposed to a more intense light for a greater part of the day than windows with any other orientation. Consequently, the light that comes through these 15th-century windows is like a trumpet blast in the otherwise complete and harmonious ensemble of the 12th and 13th centuries. It is only when one walks right up to the Vendôme windows that, shutting out all else, one can enjoy them as very creditable works of their time.

More than any other mural art the art of stained glass is affected by what is actually *there* – in the sky, in the walls, as well as in its own particular colors and forms. It is thus the most "Taoist" form of painting ever to have been developed in the Western world, and it is perhaps this more than anything else that has made the medium so hard for us to grasp.

Yet even artificial light can be coped with, as Gyorgy Kepes demonstrated in his luminous wall for the KLM Royal Dutch Airlines ticket office in New York. There, rather than make any attempt to fake daylight, Kepes made his lighting *as artificial as possible*. Behind his large black perforated wall are a variety of light circuits that blink on and off, delineating a series of different patterns, and behind a large rose-colored sunburst of slab glass are sheets of crinkled metal foil suspended in such a way that they create a marvelous shimmering effect. The result is a gaily appropriate evocation of aerial routes and of night flight over cities that altogether avoids the "drowned" look of most artificially illuminated stained glass. George Robert Lewis and Alistair and Mariette Bevington have been equally skillful in creating freestanding stained-glass constructions that are actually designed to be looked *at* as much as *through*, and to a large extent they are thus freed from dependence upon any critical balancing of inside and outside light. These are radical but absolutely valid, logical extensions of the medium.

From what has already been said it will be apparent why the nightlighting of stained-glass windows designed essentially to be seen in daylight can seldom be more than a gesture. The conditions may sometimes be such that a stained-glass window will "reverse" at night, that is, become attractively visible from the outside; but fundamentally, first and last of all, stained glass is an art that lives and breathes natural light; and it is the play of natural light, so long cherished by architects and sculptors for the infinite range of its effects, upon which stained glass even more than other arts depends for the life of its forms.

14. G. Robert Lewis: Stained-glass Construction, Hall of Glass, Museum of History and Technology, Washington, D. C., 1962.

15. and 17. Alistair Bevington: Stained-glass Space Divider,
Bankers Trust Company, New York, 1963.

Below: 16. Mariette Bevington: Free-standing Stained-glass
Panel, Yonkers, New York.

III RADIANCE

Not only must we reckon with the luminous environment of stained glass as the creator of its texture and its relative brightness; since the stained-glass window is illuminated by transmitted rather than reflected light, it possesses a range of brightness values far exceeding that possible in any opaque form of painting. To appreciate the extent of the difference, let us turn once more to the door panel illustrated in Chapter I. The room in which it is located is actually a very light room, lighter than our photograph suggests. Its walls are white and there is a large bay window just to the left of the table, another window the size of the door to its right. The stained-glass panel faces east. At nine o'clock on a clear October morning with the direct rays of the sun coming into the room from this direction, the white wall under the clock has a brightness value of approximately 1.6 c/ft.^{2}, or candles per square foot, as measured with a Weston Master exposure meter. The walnut molding that frames the door reads about half this, or .8 c/ft.^{2} At the same time, however, the *darkest* piece of glass in the door light, a piece of ruby in the lower third of the panel, reads 3.2, or twice as bright as the white wall; while the brightest piece of glass, a clear white seen against the sky in the upper right-hand corner of the window, reads 400, or 256 times as bright as the white wall!

Fully as important as this absolute difference in brightness, however, is the difference between the brightness range within the stained-glass window itself and that possible in any opaque medium. The readings for this window, 3.2 to 400 c/ft.^{2}, are in the ratio of 1 : 128. In comparison, the maximum brightness range of a glossy black-and-white photograph is, according to Ansel Adams, in the neighborhood of 1 : 50; of a print on rough dead-matte paper 1 : 20; that of a "vigorous water color only about 1 : 8, a strong painting about 1 : 10."[7] It is clear from these examples that the stained-glass artist therefore normally works with a brightness range of direct light values that may be anywhere from ten to fifteen times as great as that of the average easel painting.

What are the actual characteristics of this greatly expanded range of brightness values and intensities of light that are so much greater absolutely than they are in any other kind of painting? They are many, they are complex, and they are not altogether understood. Until recently Viollet-le-Duc's theory of color radiation and his diagrammatic analyses of the way in which 12th- and 13th-century stained-glass windows were supposedly designed to control this radiation had been generally accepted as authoritative on the whole, even by most glass painters. Blue, according to Viollet-le-Duc, tends to radiate over all other colors, and most particularly over red, when viewed at a distance.

Seemingly corroborative of the theory of blue radiation are such undisputed phenomena as the fact that the west windows of Chartres, though they contain the full palette of 12th-century colors – blue, ruby, a rich wine-pink, smoky yellow, ruddy flesh tint, green and white – seem when viewed from a distance to be essentially blue windows, the clearest, most intense imaginable blue, with all of the other colors reduced to very neutralized tints of themselves. This is an effect that often plagues the photographer of stained-glass windows at any distance. Warm pinks, for example, especially tend to take on a violet cast if they are in the vicinity of blue, regardless of the type of film used and in spite of the normal precaution of a skylight filter. Either a much warmer filter, utilization of the very warm daylight of early morning or late afternoon, or some other control in the processing of the film is often required to compensate for this over-activity of blue light.[8] Even more impressive to most glass painters, however, are the many Gothic Revival windows of the past hundred years that take on a nasty purplish glow when seen at a distance, as though the ruby and blue in them, the two predominant colors, had optically mixed in the most appalling way.

Viollet-le-Duc had thought to analyze such problems in "Vitrail" and to illustrate the principles employed by the makers of the ancient windows to control and even exploit them: "... let us imagine a design in glass," he wrote ...

worked out according to Fig. 2. The black lines indicate the leads (see A). The compartments R are red, the compartments L are blue, and the bands C white. Here is the effect that will be produced at a distance of about twenty meters (see B).

The circular blue compartments 'l' radiate as far as the dotted circles, and the red remains pure only in the middle of each compartment 'r.' The result is that all the surfaces 'o' are red tinged with blue, that is violet; that the dividing whites between the tones, not having any colored radiation of their own, are lightly tinged with blue in 'v' as are also the leads themselves; that the general effect of this glass is cold and purplish over the greater part of its surface, with spots 'r' harsh if you are close to the glass, somber if you are at a great distance away from it. Now if (see A) we diminish the field of the blue discs by black painting, as is shown in D, we neutralize partially the radiating effect of these discs. If instead of white bands C we place yellowish or greenish white bands, and if we draw lines on these bands as is shown at 'e' or beads, as at 'f,' then we obtain a much better effect. The blues, being heavily surrounded by black designs and further picked out with black internally, lose their radiating faculty. The reds are then much less tinged with violet by their proximity. The yellowish or greenish tones of the filets gain in delicacy by the blue tones which, tinting each of their ends, leave between a warm part which ties with the reds, especially if we have taken the pains to increase the value of the leads by the beading or by simple internal lines.[9]

Recently, Dr. James R. Johnson had a stained-glass panel made according to the specifications of Viollet-le-Duc's Figure 2 and observed it at the prescribed distance. Neither he nor a dozen of his colleagues saw

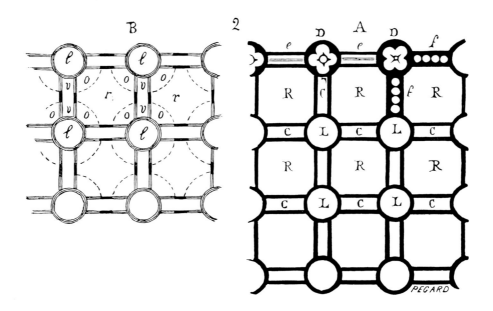

the effects described by Viollet-le-Duc: "all the colors seemed to suffer a loss in brightness, but I was not able to detect any discoloration in the reds as a result of the invasion of the blues," he informs us. "I saw no violet circumferences as a result of their juxtaposition, nor did the white strips seem to take on any blue coloration, however light. As for the blue disk made smaller by over-painting, and the white strips upon which designs were made, their visibility and brightness were reduced by this treatment, but no alteration of color was observed in other areas of the panel. The general effect of the glass did not seem cold, nor was it violet-tinged. The reds were in no way overwhelmed by the blues: rather, it appeared to be the reverse, for the dominant tonality of the panel was red, if only because this color occupied the largest surface area."[10]

Equally damaging to the credibility of Viollet-le-Duc is the fact that nowhere in this example is there any mention of the size of such a panel or of the kind of light conditions under which it is to be viewed. When Johnson deduced its most logical size from the typical size of such pieces of glass in 12th-century windows, he found himself trying to observe very subtle nuances of color on four-inch squares of ruby and one and seven-eighth-inch disks of blue glass at a distance of 20 meters or 65 feet – at a distance where even the whole panel, two feet long, became a very tiny object *in an altogether undefined visual field*. We are given no clue as to its proper setting, and a key example from "Vitrail," one that had for so long seemed especially plausible in the abstract,[11] turns out to be too vague even to be readily tested!

We are left with nothing more than a quasi-scientific explanation of such very real phenomena as the theories of color radiation in "Vitrail" had heretofore seemed to explain. Is color radiation then a function not of color as such but rather of brightness, in which case as Dr. Johnson says, "*any* spectral hue could irradiate more than others if it exceeded them in brightness"? Until someone has an opportunity to make comparative light readings of the various colors in the west windows of Chartres, or devises some equally compelling test, we cannot be sure; but a problem this well defined is seldom far from its solution.

No discussion of stained glass would be complete without some speculation about its extraordinary power to dominate a space and determine its atmosphere. It *is* true, as Herbert Read once wrote, that "no other art can be so vital, so much a part of solar life; in comparison, the blind masses of sculpture and the opaque planes of painting are void and insentient."[12] It *is* true that the best windows in the cathedrals are "at once cold and fiery – luminous as if themselves the source of light – incandescent, icy prisms, mapping the cosmology of an ideal."[13] How are we to account for this quality, this capacity of the ancient windows that so confused and exasperated even Mr. Berenson?

Recently Aldous Huxley, that intrepid voyager to what he calls "the mind's antipodes," made a fascinating comparison between the kinds of things typically seen in visionary experiences and the effect that things naturally having the same qualities have upon us all:

Every mescalin experience, every vision arising under hypnosis, is unique; but all recognizably belong to the same species. The landscapes, the architecture, the clustering gems, the brilliant and intricate patterns–these, in their atmosphere of preternatural light, preternatural color and preternatural significance, are the stuff of which the mind's antipodes are made. Why this should be so, we have no idea. It is a brute fact of experience which, whether we like it or not, we have to accept—just as we have to accept the fact of kangaroos.

From these facts of visionary experience let us now pass to the accounts preserved in all the cultural traditions, of Other Worlds—the worlds inhabited by the gods, by the spirits of the dead, by man in his primal state of innocence.

Reading these accounts, we are immediately struck by the close similarity between induced or spontaneous visionary experience and the heavens and fairylands of folklore and religion. Preternatural light, preternatural intensity of coloring, preternatural significance—these are all characteristic of all the Other Worlds and Golden Ages . . .

Indeed, we may risk a generalization and say that whatever, in nature or in a work of art, resembles one of those intensely significant, inwardly glowing objects encountered at the mind's antipodes is capable of inducing, if only in a partial and attenuated form, the visionary experience . . .

Religious art has always and everywhere made use of these vision-inducing materials. The shrine of gold, the chryselephantine statue, the jeweled symbol or image, the glittering furniture of the altar—we find these things in contemporary Europe as in ancient Egypt, in India and China as among the Greeks, the Incas, the Aztecs . . .

For the men of the Middle Ages, it is evident, visionary experience was supremely valuable. So valuable, indeed, that they were ready to pay for it in hard-earned cash. In the twelfth century collecting boxes were placed in the churches for the upkeep and installation of stained-glass windows. Suger, the Abbot of St. Denis, tells us that they were always full.[14]

Indeed, the Abbot makes it quite clear in his own writings that he is aware of this vision-inducing quality in the treasures and fabric of his church: "When —out of my delight in the beauty of the house of God — the loveliness of the many-colored stones has called me away from external cares, and worthy meditation has induced me to reflect, transferring that which is material to that which is immaterial, on the diversity of the sacred virtues: then it seems to me that I see myself dwelling, as it were, in some strange region of the universe which neither exists entirely in the slime of the earth nor entirely in the purity of Heaven; and that, by the grace of God, I can be transported from this inferior to that higher world in an anagogical manner."[15]

How versed were the actual designers of the windows in St.-Denis and Canterbury, Chartres and Bourges, with the neo-Platonic light metaphysics that, as Panofsky demonstrates, so clearly lies behind Suger's thoughts? How literate were these consummate artisans? There is an exquisite 13th-century panel in the Victoria and Albert Museum, a mate to the two reproduced on page 122, in which the name of the prophet Daniel is painted in mirror image. Is this the mistake of a man who could not read, or is it a drollery? We cannot tell. But there is no question that to the vision-inducing properties inherent in the intense light and color of stained glass these painters brought a particularly effective pattern sense, a sense of evershifting figure-and-ground relationships that in itself tends to be transporting. But of that more will be said in Chapter VIII.

A   B

IV THE FABRIC OF A STAINED-GLASS
   WINDOW

The art of stained glass is first of all an art of creating images out of
colored glass and placing them effectively before the light. It is not now
and probably never was, for the designer or glass painter, essentially the
art of staining or coloring glass. Making colored glass and making stained-
glass windows out of such glass stand in exactly the same relation as do the
manufacture of oil paints and the art of easel painting. Glass for stained-
glass windows is colored by the addition of various metal oxides, such as
iron, copper, silver, selenium or cobalt while it is in a molten state. Small
sheets of glass approximately 20 by 30 inches in size are then made from
this glass by an ancient technique – hence the name "antique." The molten
glass is gathered on a blowpipe, blown into a bubble which the glass

C   D   E

blower manipulates into a long cylindrical shape. The ends of the cylinder are cut off, it is slit down one side and gently flattened into a sheet in an annealing oven. It is with such sheets of colored glass that the art of stained-glass window making begins.

With the exceptions we shall note in due course, each separate piece of glass is therefore essentially *one color throughout*, so that when the artist wants to go from any one color to another, from ruby to blue for example, he has to go from a piece of ruby glass to a piece of blue glass and allow for a line of lead between them. The only practicable exceptions to this are the process of staining glass yellow with silver salts that can be applied like a paint and fired onto the glass, a process discovered in the 14th century, and a somewhat later process whereby the surface color is removed from "flashed" or laminated glass consisting of two colors. Of this more will be said in Chapter VI.

Our diagrams retrace the basic steps in the making of a typical 13th-century panel, *The Prophet Ezekiel*, from a French "Jesse Tree" window: from the design or cartoon (A) a pattern (B) is made, showing the exact shapes and sizes of the pieces of glass to be cut, and indicating the color for each piece, *R* for ruby, *W* for white, and so on. A piece of glass of the proper color is selected for each area and cut to shape, allowing a small space between it and all adjacent pieces for the leading, as in (C). The details of the design, in this case features, drapery and ornamental motifs, are then painted onto the glass, often literally traced from the cartoon (D). The paint used for this is a relatively colorless vitreous enamel composed of dense brownish, blackish or gray-greenish metal oxides and ground glass mixed with some purely temporary aqueous glue binder like gum arabic. This glass paint can be applied either opaquely or in thin films, to overlay the basic color of the glass with a purely tonal shading. (While much of the shading has disappeared from the earliest windows or merged with the patina on the glass, it can be clearly seen on a very early and unusually well-preserved *Head of Christ* from Wissembourg, shown on page 49.)

Right: 18. "The Prophet Ezekiel," French, 13th century; detail (approximately actual size). *Victoria & Albert Museum, Crown Copyright.*

When all of the glass has been selected, cut, painted where necessary and fired, the pieces are assembled with pre-formed strips of lead. These have an "H" cross section with grooves on either side to take the glass (E). They are fitted around all of the pieces and the joints are then soldered, first on one side of the panel, then on the other. It is then waterproofed by scrubbing or pressing a putty solution under the leads and it is ready for installation.

To this traditional technique of leaded windows we must now add the technique of assembling antique glass with epoxy resin. In its simplest form the epoxy window is patterned, cut, painted and fired in exactly the same way as the leaded window, using the same materials. But instead of being joined to one another by strips of lead the finished pieces of glass are glued to a sheet of plate glass with clear epoxy resin, as in our example in Chapter I. There is no limit to the number of layers of glass (or other materials) that may be superimposed in such a window, but since such elaborations do not change the technique in principle they need not detain us here.

The third basic technique of making stained-glass windows is also, like the epoxy technique, of recent origin and, like it, the result of a new material: cast slab glass. Whereas the glass in leaded and epoxy windows is normally about three-sixteenths of an inch thick, more or less, slab glass is cast in units that are more nearly an inch thick. Because of this even the lightest colored slabs have a very substantial appearance, which the glazier may further accentuate by flaking their surfaces. Here again the window is made by cutting the glass to a pattern; but the pieces are then laid out in precise order inside a frame of the desired panel size and concrete[16] is poured around and between all the pieces up to the desired thickness of the panel, usually the full thickness of the glass.

Many people have come to feel that slab-glass windows are the "glass-iest," or the "most contemporary," or "most architectural" stained-glass windows of all, and there is little question that this technique has greatly extended the possibilities of the medium as has the epoxy technique. Which of the three is best? It is important to understand why the question can have no meaningful answer except in relation to a particular kind of setting, particular light conditions.

The epoxy technique is the *only* practicable technique of making stained glass in which there need not be some kind of opaque skeleton surrounding and joining each separate piece of glass to its neighbors. Since the pieces of glass may abut each other directly – since there need not always be an interval of at least an eighth of an inch of lead or cement between all colors – this is inherently the highest-keyed technique of making stained glass; and in structural detailing it is also the cleanest. The individual sections of an epoxy window can be many times larger than the sections of either leaded or concrete windows without the need for framing and supporting members. They are limited in size only by the size of the plate glass that can be handled in the stained-glass studio.

Right: 19. Matthew Wysocki: Slab-glass and Concrete Window, Grace Chapel, Southport Congregational Church, Southport, Connecticut; detail.

Epoxy windows become feasible, therefore, in many places where the interior light level is much too high for either the leaded or the concrete window. Slab glass would have been inconceivable, and a leaded panel would not have worked half so well as the epoxy doorlight in our first example.

On the other hand, where sheer massiveness is desired, neither the epoxy window nor the leaded window can approach slab glass-and-concrete. Since the slab-glass panel is itself actually a piece of masonry, it easily and naturally takes its place in the masonry wall as a logical and very substantial part of it. Slab glass is really the most "expressionistic" form of stained glass, with all of its accidental, raw material aspects emphasized. How effective this technique can be in the hands of an artist with a sufficiently strong design sense can be seen from some of the examples in this book; too frequently, however, one sees slab glass made the salvation of the Disneyland medievalists of the trade, who exploit its material effects to lend a kind of spurious modernity to their work – modernity being equated with crudity. But the real limitation of slab glass aesthetically is the price that one pays for its chief virtue, its substantiality. Since slab glass is so much thicker and denser in its effect than antique glass, it cannot possibly have the liquid transparency, clarity and lightness of the latter; nor can it therefore exploit a range of diaphanous effects that will be described in Chapter V.

In spite of the new resources which slab glass and the epoxy technique have given to stained glass, the leaded window is still in many ways the most versatile and malleable technique of the three. The worst that can be said against it is that, willy-nilly, it is linked in our minds with a longer string of abuses, more "platitudes in stained-glass attitudes," than either of the more recent techniques which, moreover, still have about them the attraction of anything new. But this has not kept the better stained-glass artists from creating leaded windows that are as fresh and telling as any of those being created with the newer means. Since the leaded window has for so long proved to be an intractable medium for many of the painters who tried to work with it however, let us see where they have gone wrong, and why the recurrent strategems for "getting rid of the leads" have usually come to grief.

When we look at a typical 16th-century panel, (plate 21), we see that its thin contours and vaporous shading are everywhere at war with the much heavier, structurally irreducible lines of the leads. Where the latter follow the drawing, they over-reinforce it; where they desert it, as in the left hand of the foreground figure, the effect is even more disastrous. In the 18th century Sir Joshua Reynolds sought to eliminate this conflict not by strengthening the opacity of his drawing but by eliminating the leading altogether – only to have his armatures become prison bars that, when they occasionally deign to bend with a knee or flow with the drapery, become positively fatuous. In the recent windows of Chagall, even though there is none of the conflict between the medium and an imposed nat-

Left: 20. Fernand Leger: Slab Glass and Sanctuary Decoration, Audincourt; detail.

21. "The Last Supper," French, 16th century; detail. *Victoria & Albert Museum, Crown Copyright.*

40

22. Sir Joshua Reynolds: "The Virtues,"
New College Chapel, Oxford, 1778.

uralism that has always been taken to be the chief fault of post-medieval glass, we find lead patterns as obtrusive as those of the renaissance panel, armatures as uncertain in their irregular displacement as those in Reynolds' windows. The shortcomings of the Jerusalem windows are all the more instructive therefore, and too copiously documented by Chagall's preliminary designs for us to pass them by.

In several ways Chagall must have seemed the ideal artist to make the stained glass for a new synagogue in Israel. His Bible illustrations are unsurpassed in our time for their richness and depth of feeling; the folk fantasies of his Russian-Jewish village origins have always been a popular and endearing theme in his art; and he has always been a rich colorist. Paradoxically, it is the last of these qualifications that caused all of his trouble, for there are two radically different ways of thinking about color in painting and only one of them is really compatible with the medium of stained glass. In a word, colors may be handled so that they mean themselves and the absolute relations between themselves as they do in the work of Leger, Stuart Davis or Albers, or they may be handled in a more "painterly" fashion, so that they take on the atmospheric connotations that they have in the works of such painters as Bonnard, Chagall and even certain "abstract impressionists." Though the "painterly" approach to color is in a certain sense more colorful than the other – more iridescent – it is altogether too complex a quality to be translated into stained glass. This is true not only because its richness is achieved at the expense of clearly articulated color *areas*, which poses some very difficult problems technically, but because *its atmospheric depth is as incompatible with the actual depth effects of stained glass as the illusionistic third dimension imposed upon the medium in the Renaissance.* All other things being equal, the atmospheric

41

23. Marc Chagall: "The Tribe of Naphtali," Hadassah-Hebrew University Medical Center, Jerusalem, 1959–61.

24. Preliminary study for "The Tribe of Naphtali." *Photograph: Horizon.*

colorist is the very last kind of painter who should undertake to design stained glass, for no matter how good he may be, all of his resources go against the grain of the medium and vice versa. One need only compare Chagall's designs with the stained-glass cartoons of Leger and Matisse to realize how much more at home with the medium the latter were than Chagall, or for that matter Rouault or Abraham Rattner, could ever be.

For all that, Chagall's windows are not the kind of "mail-order modern" stained glass that frequently results from such commissions. Chagall took the trouble to learn the techniques of glass painting and to get everything out of his designs that could be gotten out of them by painting the windows himself. Some of the details are thus very charming, pure Chagall; and yet one hardly needs to see his preliminary sketches to know that these windows were simply not conceived in terms of stained glass. In the series of four studies exhibited for each window one finds absolutely no evolution toward *stained glass;* in those actually labelled "final," only the most tentative indications even of the armatures; and when the leading was actually plotted – not by the artist at all, apparently, but by

25. A stained-glass cartoon and preliminary sketches in Matisse's studio, Hotel Regina, Nice, 1953.

26. Leger with his cartoons for the Audincourt windows.

his collaborator, Charles Marq – it was tretaed, as one critic remarked, like an overscaled "craquelure."[17] The irony is that fifty years ago, when Chagall painted his great canvas, *I and the Village*, his approach to color and form was much more compatible with stained glass than it has since become. What a pity he could not have gotten his great stained-glass commissions then!

If Chagall may be said to have failed to master the medium through a kind of ingenuousness, there are others who have been all too clever in incorporating the leading in their imagery. I have in mind the kind of thing one sees in a *Composition* by Fritz Winter. Why this great effort to "swallow up" the leading altogether so that in a photograph one hardly knows that one is looking at stained glass at all? Or one sees in Meistermann's window for the Darmstadt Museum another questionable tendency, a forcing of the kind of shapes that can be cut from glass. Since glass is a brittle, grainless material, it is cut by simply scoring its surface with a common wheel cutter, as for example along the axis AA in our diagram, and then cracking it where it has been thus weakened. But the structure

27. Fritz Winter: "Composition," 1957.

28. Lead and armature pattern of a stained-glass window in Les Bréseux by Manessier, with ironwork executed by the local foundry. *L'Art Sacré*.

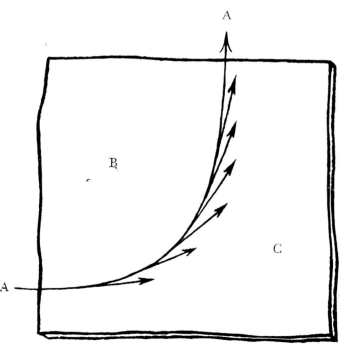

29. Georg Meistermann: Stained-glass Window, Darmstadt Museum, 1959.

30. G. Robert Lewis: Sacristy Windows, Church of the Messiah, Glens Falls, New York.

of glass is such that when it is cracked, the crack wants at every point to continue in a straight line. Thus it is far easier to cut a convex shape (B) out of such a piece of glass, allowing (C) to come away in fragments, than it is to cut the concave shape (C) by breaking away (B); and the more acute the changes of direction in a concavity, the more difficult they are to cut. To anyone who has actually worked with glass, such sharply notched pieces as the one in the center of Meistermann's window are rather painful; one readily imagines them snapping under the stress of wind pressure or sudden radical temperature changes (although, to be sure, some scarcely less involuted pieces have survived intact from the Middle Ages).

How much is ever gained by such forcing of the medium? In Meistermann's handsome composition it is a kind of implied depth-by-overlapping, an illusion that one would not wish to see carried any further in this medium even if glass were the most malleable of materials. If there is an irreducible strain of Prometheanism in our souls, one wonders why it is so seldom expressed in stained glass with the aplomb of Lewis's sacristy windows in Glens Falls?

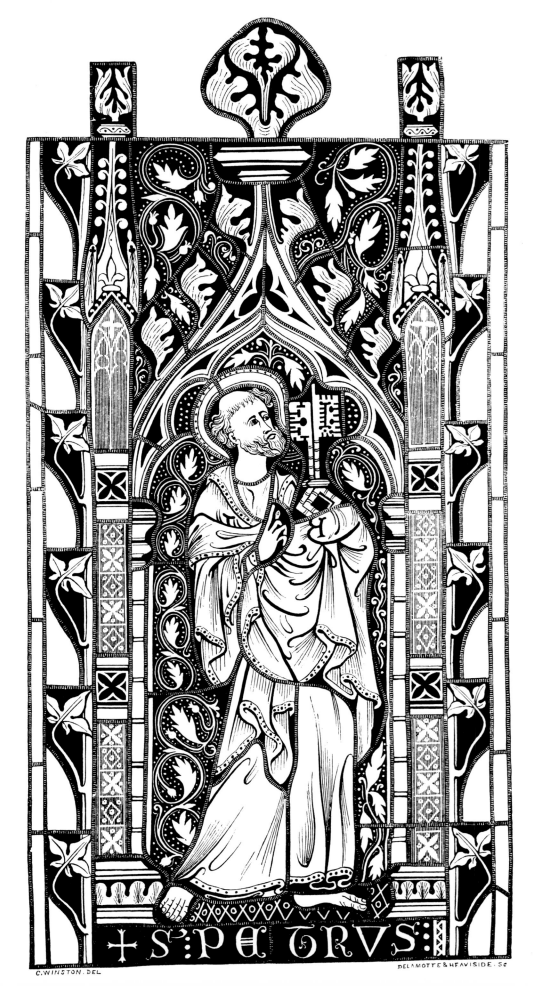

"St. Peter," Stamford Church, Northamptonshire. *Plate 12 from Charles Winston's Hints on Glass Painting.*

V THE PRINCIPLES OF GLASS PAINTING

To put it in the simplest terms the art of glass painting consists of manipulating a colorless mud on the surface of colored glass in such a way as to break up, mute, or altogether block in places the light that comes through it. Effective glass painting presupposes and completes a viable organization of all the other elements – colors, leadlines, bars and mullions – that as we have already seen must function visually as well as structurally. If we look at the diagram of a canopied 14th-century *St. Peter*, we see how its solidly painted masses and lines are masterfully fused with the leading in the final image. The leading is neither flaunted nor altogether hidden; rather it is masterfully "lost" and "found" throughout the design.

When used as a halftone, glass painting may be anything from the simplest "smear" shading of the 12th century to the over-elaborate modelling one sees in 18th-century windows, anything from a means of muting over-brilliant colors to an excessively illusionistic device. As long as artists were obsessed with the conquest of naturalistic forms, they were unable to conceive of glass painting as anything but a singularly intractable form of easel painting. But now that contemporary art has taught us once again to read the expressive nuances of every variety of "raw nature," we are in a position to appreciate the most essential, elementary beauty of the painted halftone in stained glass. Antique glass is, as we have already seen, an extremely rich transparent material in itself, given the proper background. When we apply halftones to its surfaces, we create translucent areas which react altogether differently to a differentiated light source than do the transparent areas. The difference is most clearly seen not in stained glass but in Victorian cut, sanded, or embossed glass where the whole effect of ornamentation is created through the manipulation of just these two qualities on a single piece of colorless glass.

Notice how the translucent field of frosted glass underlying the floral motifs in our example tends to hold its middle tone value in spite of the extreme light changes outside the window, while the design embossed upon it, which is much more nearly transparent, takes on the tonality of whatever is directly beyond any part of it. In the center of the panel the embossed floral motifs thus read as light-on-dark, while at the edges they read as dark-on-light; and in the presence of the actual panel this reversal of values has no fixed position but as many variations as the ever-shifting

32. "Head of Christ," Wissembourg,
11th–12th century, Strasbourg Museum.

play of light and shade outside can give it. The same magnificent chiaroscuro is at the disposal of the glass painter once he learns how to exploit the relatively static translucency of his painted halftones and the mercurial variability of his unpainted, transparent glass. The way the *Head of Christ* from Wissembourg is painted suggests that the glass painters of the 12th century must have been perfectly aware of this phenomenon, for if viewed against a comparably variegated background, its unpainted areas and its halftones would produce a similar effect. For the first time in five hundred years no overwhelming barrier of taste stands between the artist and this purest kind of glass painting.

Before the novice tries to master the many valid techniques of glass painting, he would do well to study the following observations drawn from the writings of Charles Winston. A lawyer by profession, Winston became enamored with medieval stained glass in England in the 1840's. He made many extraordinarily sensitive drawings of ancient windows – far less "Victorian" in their drawing than many of the actual restorations of the time[18] – cataloguing the characteristic features of each succeeding period; he had samples of the old glass chemically analyzed and was largely instrumental in reviving the manufacture of antique glass in England; and he lectured and wrote extensively on the art. His first book, as its leisurely title tells us, was *An Inquiry into the Difference of Style Observable in Ancient Glass Paintings, especially in England; with Hints on Glass Painting, by an Amateur*.[19] Among his hints on glass painting are these very essential formulations which we are now able to document, as Winston was not, with photographic details of the ancient windows:

Stained glass will be dull, if its lights be not kept clear and bright, whether its shadows be strong or weak; opaque if its shadows be not transparent, notwithstanding the brilliancy of its lights, and heavy if the aggregate volume of the shadows greatly exceeds that of the lights . . .

A coat of enamel brown smeared smoothly and evenly on the glass will exclude the light more completely in this state than after it has been rendered irregular in its texture by the process of stippling. For this process collects the color into little lumps or dots, leaving interstices between them less loaded with color, and consequently more pervious to the rays of light than any part of the ground before it is stippled. A stipple shadow is therefore always more transparent than a smear shadow of equal depth . . .

The ancient artists appear never to have applied more than two coats of enamel to the same side of the glass. They seem to have first spread a thin stipple ground of enamel brown all over the glass, and after having cleared the bright lights out of it, to have heightened the depth of the shadow by a thicker coat of colour . . . This second coat was very coarsely stippled, and it would seem as if its moisture softened the first coat, and caused it also to be disturbed by the stippling; for the stippling of the second coat appears, in all the specimens I have examined, to have gone right through to the glass. This causes the stipple shadows of an ancient glass painting to be in general clearer and more transparent than those of a modern glass painting, which are usually composed of several distinct coats of paint, some not infrequently being applied after the others have been actually burnt in: a practice which has a tendency to fill up the lighter interstices of the ground, and to counteract the effects of stippling.

This was the procedure of the 15th century especially, the artists of earlier centuries having confined themselves to the more or less rudimentary smear shading that we see in the Wissembourg *Head of Christ*. However, it was often modulated much more subtly than it is in that panel. Such shading is exceedingly hard to photograph since it is so delicate that one loses it in exposing for the darker colors. Traces of it are visible, however, in our 13th-century *Ezekiel* panel (page 35) and the 14th-century *Virgin* from Oxford (page 55). In our much enlarged detail of the 15th-century head of *St. James* the glass seems to have been stippled overall with some slight deepening of the shadow areas, applied as Mr. Winston suggests. The sharp highlights were evidently scratched into the halftone last of all, since they cut through even the line drawing in several places.

The following observations are from Winston's *Memoirs*, a posthumous collection of his letters and lectures published in 1865:[20]

The style of your ornamentation must, in my opinion, be regulated by the texture of your material; for if there is one point more thoroughly established than another

Right: 33. "Head of St. James the Great," 15th century; detail enlarged, *Victoria & Albert Museum*.

34. "Hezekiah and the Sundial of Ahaz," Canterbury, c. 1200.

Right: 35. "Grisaille" Window, Lincoln Cathedral, 13th century; detail.

in point of fact, it is that in ancient glass the style of ornamentation and treatment of the material varied with the texture of the material. And this was artistic enough, because a powerful material neither required, nor indeed would show, any very delicate ornamentation or soft shading; whereas a weaker sort of glass required more painter's manipulation to give it force; and paintings executed in it in the same way as in the earlier ones would have looked thin and miserable.[21]

... as idleness is the root of mischief, I propose to give you a Chapter on *Dirt*, if that is not a misnomer, the authoritative definition of the subject being "matter in the wrong place."

The question of "la patina" has engaged my attention for some time ... No manipulation that would not be destructive of the painting will produce the same broken effect that time produces ... the effect of age is *plus* all efforts of art: it softens what would otherwise be harsh, without necessarily impairing the painting. This is exemplified in those windows at King's College, Cambridge, which have been cleaned. The black dirt which obscured or interfered with the painting has been removed; but the lighter discoloration, the *beeswing* of age, still remains and softens all the flat parts; and the difficulty has always been how to produce this admirable effect by artificial means ...

In all English and French glass that I have seen *antiquated*, the process has been to bedaub the whole individual piece, and then to rub away some of the dirt in the center of the piece; whereas nature bedaubs the center of the piece, leaving, in general, the edges comparatively clear. The effect in the former case is, when the pieces of glass are very small, to make the whole design look as if it were *greasy* – as if it were made up of lumps of different-coloured fats, each lump having its own proper highlight, like the little dumplings one sees swimming about in mutton broth ...[22]

Winston then goes on to describe a rather ingenious procedure for "antiquing" modern glass (which the reader must get from Winston himself, since I do not want to appear to be recommending it. The value of this whole statement quite apart from the pros and cons of faking the dirt of the ages in modern windows is Winston's acute awareness of the actual character of ancient glass in its present state, of the actual effects of age upon its appearance.) He continues:

This dirtying is of little use unless the material itself (i.e., the glass used) resembles the old in texture ...

Here endeth the chapter on Dirt. You will understand I advocate its use with great caution and art, so as to improve what is already good in colour, tone, and drawing, not as a substitute for any or all of these things, as some of our glasswrights employ it.[23]

I have discovered a simple mode of testing whether, on the one hand, glass is sufficiently opaque, so as not to appear flimsy or watery when put up in a window unassisted by shading, according to the flat style of glass-painting; on the other, whether it is sufficiently clear to produce as brilliant an effect as the old one does. It is this: if the glass, held at arm's-length from the eye, and at a distance of *more* than a yard from an object, does not permit of that object being distinctly seen through it, the glass will be sufficiently opaque; and if, when held at the same distance from the eye, and at a distance of *not* more than a yard from the object, it permits of the latter being distinctly seen through the glass, it will be sufficiently clear and transparent. I have found this to be the case with a great many pieces of glass of the twelfth, thirteenth, and fourteenth centuries, which had been rendered clear by polishing the surface, or which were already quite clear; for it is a great mistake to suppose that all old glass has been rendered dull on the surface by exposure to the atmosphere.[24]

Right: 36. "The Virgin," Christ Church, Oxford, 14th century; detail.

. . . glass painters are led to value ancient glass paintings only so far as they supply a means of making copies; instead of endeavouring to penetrate into their principles, and found upon them a new and consistent style of glass-painting – an object for which the ancient examples are deserving of the closest study.[25]

Even though one might now choose deliberately to employ some of the effects that Winston disallowed, this in no way detracts from the value of his observations, for he was an exemplary critic who perceived the qualities and described the techniques of ancient glass painting at a time when Gothic painting was still almost universally deplored for the "crudity" of its technique. In glass painting as in all else how to do it is inseparable from how to *see* it, and there is no more reliable guide to the art of glass painting than Winston and the ancient windows, regardless of one's own style or intentions.

VI THE VARIETIES OF GLASS

We have already had occasion in Chapter IV to describe the two basic kinds of glass used in making stained-glass windows: antique glass and cast slab glass. In addition to these there are a number of special kinds of glass which can be employed to achieve the particular effects that our descriptions of them will indicate.

"Seedy" antique is simply a very bubbly antique. The bubbles make this glass noticeably more brilliant than regular antique since they catch and scatter the light, and for the same reason less transparent – often a most useful property. "Reamy" antique is a glass that has been made more than usually irregular in texture during the process of its manufacture. Most important of all, however, are the various "flashed" glasses, which are laminates of two different colors, usually a clear white or softly tinted base color upon which a thin film of a much more intense color has been flashed during the process of its manufacture. Flashed colors on clear glass often have a particular clarity or, where one color is flashed on the tint of its complement, such as ruby-on-green, a fine subtlety; and flashed glass may in addition be regular, seedy, reamy or "streaky," in which latter case the flash runs thicker and thinner on the base, making for a noticeable shading in its color. Where a ruby flash runs thin on a greeny base one often gets marvelously rich browns and auburns.

But the special values of flashed glass are two: first, since any degree or part of the flash may be removed from the base color with hydrofluoric acid, the artist is able to produce any number of effects with the *two* colors, the flash and the base, on a single piece of glass. Aciding, together with the yellow stain that can be painted and fired onto the glass, thus provides the artist with the means of creating a still limited but considerable range of transparent color variations on a single piece of glass, quite apart from the gamut of tonal values that can be created with glass paint. It is easy to be seduced by these various means into striving for effects that would make the execution of a large window not only inordinately time–consuming and expensive, but would be largely lost if not absolutely detrimental to its effect at a distance. One should never forget that colored light mixes additively toward white light as the sum of all colors, and the artist has to reckon with the serious possibility of creating windows that, however rich they may be in detail close at hand, create a very weak pastel-colored impression overall. For this reason alone, inherent in the

37. Theresa Obermayr: stained-glass panel made entirely of flashed blue glass acided painted and stained, 1952.

38. Robert Sowers: "Red One," 1952; detail.

physical behavior of light, the "gemmaux" technique in which granulated colored glass is employed is essentially non-architectural.

The second important property of flashed glass is the result of combining a clear color either in the base or the flash with an opal, or milk, glass in the other. Normally the most brilliant colors in stained-glass windows read as a completely neutral tone on the exterior. If an intense light color is flashed with a film of opal glass, however, two things happen: depending upon the thickness of the flash the glass becomes to a greater or lesser degree less transparent, and some of the color is reflected back toward the light source – a fraction of its color becomes visible on the *exterior*. If on the other hand an intense color is flashed on an opal *base*, that color will be reflected back toward its light source in its full brilliance, and inside it will glow through the opal base to some degree, depending upon the interior light level. By combining opal-flashed antiques and color-flashed opals with the traditional antique colors in varying proportions one can actually "reverse" the stained-glass window, give it whatever amount of exterior color value seems architecturally desirable.

In addition to the common units of slab glass that are cast in rectangular *dalles* approximately two-thirds of a square foot in area, we may note

39. Robert Sowers: flashed opal, opal-flashed antique and antique glass mural, American Airlines Terminal, Kennedy International Airport, New York; Kahn & Jacobs, Architects, Roy Bent Associate, 1958–59.

40. Jean-Luc Perrot: slab-glass and concrete window made of dalles de Boussois, Church of St. Joan of Arc, near Belfort.

41. Dominikus Böhm: mechanical glass in the baptistery windows, Church of Maria Königin, Cologne, 1953.

42. Baptistery and Nave Wall, exterior, Church of Maria Königin.

the giant slabs produced by Boussois of France in various shapes and sizes as large as ten square meters per slab. These make possible such large-scale, almost Gargantuan effects as one sees exploited by Jean-Luc Perrot in his windows for the Church of St. Joan of Arc in Belfort.

The final type of glass that we will consider – on the strength of its very imaginative use in one instance alone – is rolled and pressed mechanical glass, the kind of glass that one normally associates with office partitions and shower doors. In the Church of Maria Königin in Cologne a whole wall of stained glass is composed of muted gray and lightly opal-flashed antique glass save for an occasionally delicate cluster of color, and in the baptistery a similar window encloses the space – similar in color but tighter in pattern. Perhaps a quarter of the glass in the baptistery windows is me-

43. Dominikus Böhm and Heinz Bienefeld: Stained-glass Wall of the Nave, Church of Maria Königin, Cologne, 1953.

chanical glass; in any event it picks up a myriad variety of lights and darks from the park-like surroundings in the same way that the antique glass does, only more so, or on a much larger scale, since the light-catching facets of mechanical glass are much larger in scale than the surface irregularities of antique glass. The result is a jewel-studded veil of glass suspended between the viewer and the out-of-doors, a veil that shimmers and sparkles with every slight movement that either he or the leaves on the trees outside make.

44. Hermann Gottfried: "Blüte und Strauch, preiset den Herrn," Choir Window, St. Mary's Church, Düren, 1957.

45. H. G. von Stockhausen: "Crossing the Red Sea," St. Magni, Braunschweig, 1961.

46. and 48. (right) Michel Martens: "Jerusalem Celeste," Chapel of the College of Notre Dame, Antwerp; Paul Felix, Architect. *Photographs: Art d'Eglise.*

47. Michel Martens: Le Monastère de Clarisses, Ostende; Paul Felix, Architect. *Photograph: Art d'Eglise.*

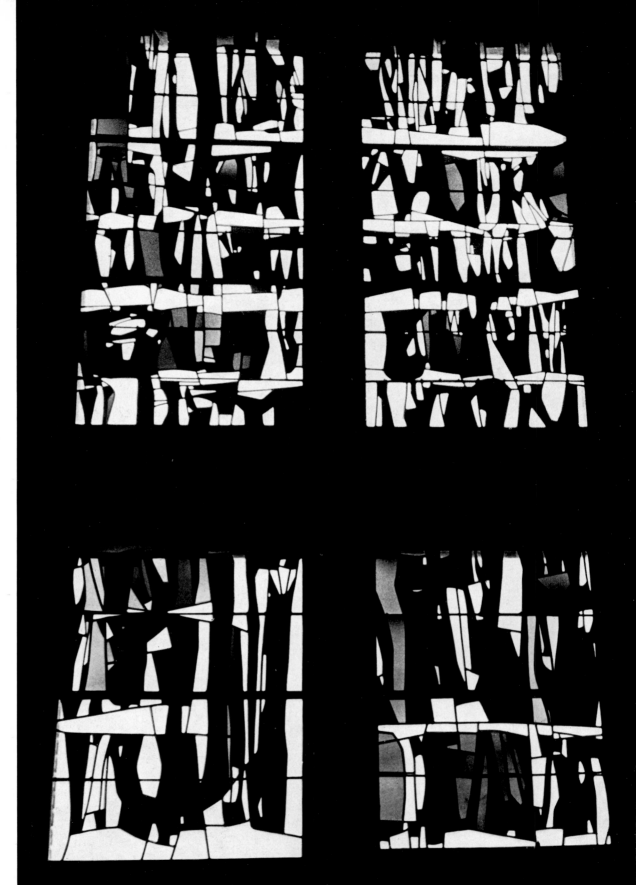

49. Gérard Lardeur:
Eglise de Prouville
(Somme).

Right: 50. Gérard Lardeur: Window for the Left Side, "Civitas Dei" Pavilion, Brussels Fair. *Photograph: Art d'Eglise.*

51. Wilhelm Buschulte: "Choir of Nine Angels," Altar Window in the Catholic Church, Stadtlohn, 1962. *Photograph: Das Münster.*

52. Wilhelm Buschulte:
St. Ursula's Church,
Cologne, 1963.

54. Avigdor Arikha: Congregation B'nai Israel, Woonsocket, Rhode Island; Samuel Glaser Associates, Architects. *Photograph: Art International.*

Left: 53. Wilhelm Buschulte: Choir Windows, St. Foillan, Aachen, 1958.

55. Ludwig Schaffrath: "Laurentius Epitaph," 1962.

Right: 56. Ludwig Schaffrath: Ursulinenkloster St. Angela, Wipperfürth; H. and E. W. Richter, Architects, 1962.

57. François Chapuis: Hall of Honor at the color works, Limoges; Harchaw-Coiffe-Rhône Poulenc, Architects.

Right: 58. Efrem Weitzman: Bellerose Jewish Center, New York; Daniel Schwartzman, Architect.

60. Robert Sowers: Stephens College Chapel, Columbia, Missouri; Eero Saarinen, Architect.

Left: 59. Albin Elskus: Pius XII School Chapel, Chester, New York.

61. Matthew Wysocki: The Chapel Window, First Presbyterian Church, Stamford, Connecticut; Sherwood, Mills & Smith, Architects.

Right: 62. Maria Katzgrau: St. Anna, Duisburg.

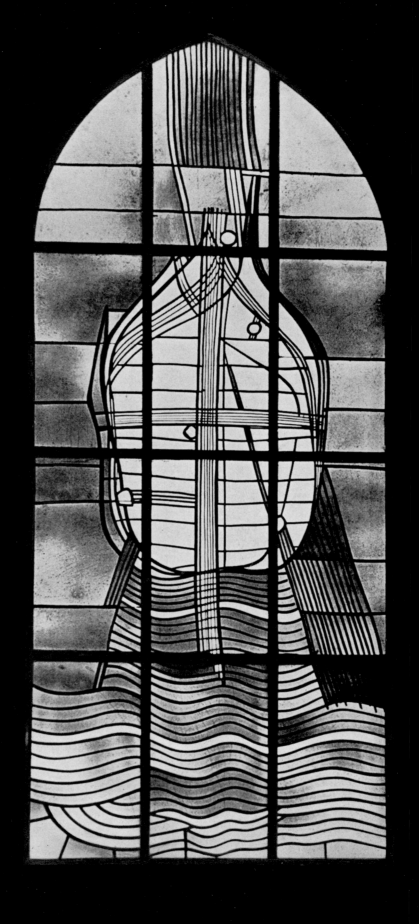

63. Georg Meistermann:
"Pascal Window," Würzburg,
1957.

PART TWO: STAINED GLASS AND CONTEMPORARY ARCHITECTURE

"The limits of the decorative can be precisely defined only in an age of humanistic art."
André Malraux

64. Sculpture Court of the German Pavilion, International Exposition, Barcelona, with standing nude by Georg Kolbe; Mies van der Rohe, Architect, 1929. *Photograph courtesy The Museum of Modern Art, New York.*

VII THE PROBLEM OF ARCHITECTURAL ART

As long as our primary concern was to define the effective properties of stained glass as a medium, we were justified in simply assuming its relation to contemporary architecture – assuming that such a relation exists and that it is valid. But at a time when many of our best architects and artists as well as critics are convinced that the integration of the arts and architecture is no longer possible, this is a generous assumption. For stained glass is so inextricably bound up with its architectural setting that if they are right, stained glass, lost or found, would be a *dead* art.

Even though the works illustrated in this volume are eloquent testimony to the contrary, this general conclusion is too common and too persistent to be readily dismissed. Granted the many very real difficulties involved in any collaborative creation – social and economic as well as aesthetic – I would like to suggest that what lies behind this conclusion is not only a series of half-hearted and thus abortive efforts to integrate art and architecture, but the example of a very successful and seemingly alternative solution to the problem of how to relate them, a solution epitomized by the Kolbe nude in the Barcelona Pavilion.

Indeed, the photograph reproduced here has become, for many people, almost the archetypal image and demonstration of what they regard as the "contemporary" relation between art and architecture. Art has become ever more individualistic and private in its imagery, they reason, while architecture has become ever more machine-like and impersonal in its character. This is a fact of our times. In some ways it is a very exciting fact, and we should try as Mies van der Rohe did to express this very difference between our art and our architecture. Along with this case for the *juxtaposition* of art and architecture goes an argument against their integration: the integration of the arts, in the words of Ada Louise Huxtable, "implies the successful fusion of architecture, the arts and the crafts into a harmonious, homogeneous whole, as we have known it in the past. Its objectives are unimpeachable and its moral tone is lofty, but it is full of fallacies for our day. In pursuing this false ideal, with our eye firmly on earlier achievements, we are rushing blindly down a dead-end street – denying the elementary truth that the 20th century revolution in all of the arts has affected not only their content and form *but their traditional relationship to each other as well*."[26]

Mies's classic achievement seems all the more remarkable when we discover that he had actually had a Lehmbruck in mind for his Pavilion: "When this proved impossible to arrange," so Peter Blake tells us, Mies "grabbed a taxi on one of his last days in Berlin before leaving for Barcelona, drove out to Kolbe's studio, and borrowed the best substitute he could find . . . Although the success of the Kolbe in this classic court does not prove that collaboration between artists and architects is unnecessary," Mr. Blake concludes, "it does suggest that there may be other and better ways toward the integration of the arts."[27] Yes and no. Less harum-scarum in realization certainly, but hardly more *well-conceived*. For the only reason that Mies could find, and happened in fact to find so adequate a substitute for the Lehmbruck at the last minute, was because *the role that the statue was to play in the Barcelona Pavilion was a clearly established part of his conception from the start*. Given such a clear-cut architectural requirement any number of nudes from the Hellenistic period onwards could have been "found" for this space. Mies's achievement was therefore less radically new, far less a purely architectural conception to which an alien form was somehow "juxtaposed," than we are inclined to assume.

Let us turn now to a work that, in the same sense as the placement of the Kolbe in the Barcelona Pavilion was a creation of the architect, was a creation of the artist: the mural that Matisse painted for the Barnes Foundation. It is a truly architectural image created for an existing space and a very difficult space at that. The space consisted of three lunettes in Barnes's central picture gallery, approximately fifteen feet high and all but separated at their bases by the soffits of the pendentives. Beneath are three tall windows that look out on the grounds, and on the walls of the gallery hang several major paintings from the collection – Cézannes, Renoirs, a Seurat, a Picasso and one of Matisse's own canvases. Thus, as Alfred Barr says, "Matisse had to meet the handicap of an awkward perspective and the competition both of nature, seen through the bright windows, and art in the form of some of the greatest masterpieces of the past hundred years of painting."[28]

We know from Matisse's own statements that he immediately recognized and accepted the limitations imposed by the nature and function of the gallery. "It is a room for paintings," he is quoted as saying. "To treat my decoration like another picture would be out of place. My aim has been to translate paint into architecture, to make of the fresco the equivalent of stone or cement. This, I think, is not often done anymore. The mural painter today makes pictures, not murals." In order to be sure of his forms in an unaccustomed scale Matisse composed his mural full-size, on the canvas itself. "My mural," he later wrote, "is the result of a physical encounter between the artist and some fifty-two square meters of surface of which the spirit of the artist has had to take possession . . ."[29] When the first version of the mural was finished it turned out to be the wrong size; a mistake had been made in the measurement of the wall. As Barr says, "After over a year's work a lesser, or a less precise, artist might have made a few minor adjustments and passed on to some less tedious undertaking. But Matisse, instead began all over again, moved in part by Dr. Barnes' apologies and eager exhortations."

Matisse painted a second, even finer version of the mural and installed it in the gallery. "As soon as I saw the decoration in place I felt that it was detached absolutely from myself, and that it took on a meaning quite different from what it had had in my studio, when it was only a painted canvas," Matisse observed. "There in the Barnes Foundation it became a rigid thing, heavy as stone, and one that seemed to have been spontaneously created at the same time as the building . . ."[30]

What do we learn from this wholly successful work? First, the space allotted to Matisse, however difficult it may have been to work with, was from an architectural point of view a very logical, not to say traditional, space for a mural decoration; and given such a space the artist may work as validly in a completed building as Mies van der Rohe worked with Kolbe's nude in the Barcelona Pavilion. Second, whether the artist can, like Matisse, see and accept the logic of such a space depends finally upon his *sense of scale*. Even though Matisse worked on his mural for a long time, from the end of 1930 until May 1933, it is evident that he had a natural feeling for the grand simplification, a feeling that was to make itself manifest again in his last great collages – a magnificent series of murals without walls, unparalleled in the whole history of modern art. Third, given this sense of scale the artist may create works that, like the Barnes mural, are no less true to the artist's own feeling for being superbly architectural. Fourth, such a sense of scale is therefore as indispensable from the artist's point of view as from the architect's, for without it the artist's most conscientious effort can satisfy neither himself nor the requirements of the space for which it is intended.

But how many artists nowadays have such a feeling for architectural art, it will be asked? Are not the Barnes mural and such other examples as one can point to simply the exceptions that prove the rule? Such works may well be created from time to time, and bravo! But let us not while away our time waiting for such century plants to bloom. Basically, the integration of the arts is foreign to the conditions of our time, foreign to our abilities, foreign even to our innermost desires. On some such argument as this the case against the integration of the arts must finally rest; and insofar as it is an argument against nostalgia, against a mere desire to emulate the past, the argument must be accepted hands down by all whose interest in the arts is more than retrospective.

Yet when we look at what is happening in the arts of our time in order to guess where our innermost desires are actually leading us, what do we find? That the paintings of Clyfford Still and Mark Rothko and their followers are suddenly seen – in spite of the artist's intentions – as "environmental objects"; that sculpture becomes increasingly "painterly" and painting begins to incorporate every conceivable object. That architecture becomes more and more consciously "sculptural" and a distinguished architect, Paul Rudolph, begins to talk about the need for a distinction between "foreground" and "background" buildings; that an architectural critic, Peter Blake, concludes that "the hero of the future must be the city itself" rather than a single building.[31] Obviously, the traditional boundaries between the arts are more unsettled now than they have been for a very long time. This is a singularly unpropitious moment for wholesale judgments or generalizations about the autonomy or ultimate separateness of any of the arts.

The argument against the integration of the arts is false in its conclusions because it is too sweeping in its premises. If *everything* cannot be integrated as in the past, it asserts, *nothing* can be integrated at all. To take such a position in the face of an increasing body of successfully integrated art and architecture is either to fly in the face of the facts or to rule out all such works by definition, a premise that becomes increasingly meaningless with each exception. One wonders why those artists and architects who

65. Harris and Ros Barron: Concrete Relief, Hartford Jewish Community Center, West Hartford, Connecticut; Walter Gropius and Norman Fletcher of Architects Collaborative, Architects.

66. Mateo Manaure: Tile Mural, City University, Caracas; C. R. Villanueva, Architect. *Photograph: Arts.*

67. William King: Bronze, walnut and incised marble frieze, Bankers Trust Company, New York.

simply dislike the idea, or cannot imagine themselves working collaboratively, cannot simply leave it at that?

More curious however is the fact that their argument usually implies a far too limited and "classical" standard of unity – a kind of unity that is not to be found in many of the greatest works of the past or present. What heterogeneous architectural elements combine to create the Piazza San Marco, or the Cathedral of Canterbury with its 12th-century choir, 14th-century nave and 15th-century towers; and what amazingly poignant inconsistencies there are even in such individual creations as Michelangelo's Rondanini *Pietà*, or Picasso's *Les Demoiselles d'Avignon* and his portrait of Gertrude Stein! As E. M. Forster once said, "Though proportion is the final secret, to espouse it from the outset is to insure sterility."

Not only does this prevalent attitude betray a kind of Beaux-Arts fastidiousness, but in an age of field theories it is based on a far too rigid concept of *things;* it is blind to the many different kinds of entities that result when any given set of elements is seen in different contexts. Only at a distance, for example, does the Empire State Building detach itself from its surroundings to become the famous landmark on the postcards. At the corner of Fifth Avenue and 34th Street *that* Empire State Building scarcely exists. There, unless one determinedly singles it out, it is but one element in a civic interior of indefinite height, a continuous composition or cacaphony of elements that runs along the streets and unfolds before one's eyes like a kind of three-dimensional scroll painting. There, a sculptured frieze may be more validly related to some lobby than that lobby can possibly be related to the twenty stories above it; there, a wrecker's scaffolding of old doors may quite accidentally assume the character of an architecture far handsomer than that coming down or that scheduled to go up in its place. In the realm of collage a famous photograph of Jackson Pollock at work on a painting merges quite fantastically with that of a Yorkshire landscape.

The relations between spaces, between forms, between images, between creations in one medium and in another are simply what they are and where we find them. Or create them.

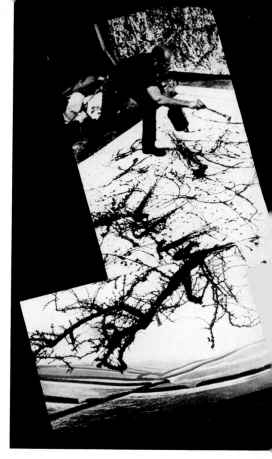

68. Photomontage.

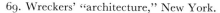

69. Wreckers' "architecture," New York.

70. "The Prophet
Ezekiel," French,
13th century.
*Victoria & Albert
Museum, Crown
Copyright.*

88

VIII STAINED GLASS AS AN ARCHITECTURAL ELEMENT

Let us now see how a typical 13th-century stained-glass window actually managed to serve at once its highly narrative, didactic function and its very ornamental, architectural function so well. If we look at a diagram of the *Ezekiel* panel, we see that its two major colors, ruby and blue, are deployed with a calculated spatial ambiguity. Since only one basic shade of ruby and one of blue were used throughout, the artist was able at once to create a sufficiently representational space and yet keep it "flat." The blue that we read as a background for Ezekiel is brought forward into the floral motifs just above and below him and then drops behind the border motifs to the left; the ruby that frames the space in which Ezekiel stands is divided only by a thin band of white from more of the same ruby that suddenly drops behind the blue floral motifs above and below the figure; and finally, Ezekiel is depicted as though he were about to step out of his space. Insofar as the panel is representational, it is ornamentally composed and calligraphically painted; though the field in which the narrative medallion is placed is purely ornamental, its elements are quasi-representational. There is thus no definite point at which the representational quality actually begins or ends, and no part of it which is not therefore absolutely compatible with the overall ornamental character of the original *Jesse Tree* window of which this panel is but a small fragment.

In such endless inversions whereby each part is imbued with the quality of its opposite, where each level of organization assumes some of the characteristics of the next, the artists of the period had perfected a means whereby one layer of imagery could be superimposed upon another, and another upon that with cumulative force. Not only were the narrative medallions deployed ornamentally in the windows, but the armatures that supported the glass began to imply the next larger, structural order of the wall itself, just as the lyricism of the windows was carried over into the detailing of the stonework. The sculpture of the portals, though endlessly subtle in detail, is grouped architecturally, while the towers of the cathedral were treated sculpturally; the manifold variety of silhouettes of the cathedral is resolved in its overall monumentality. The cathedral became a focal point in its man-made environment and a landmark on the horizon.

There is nothing mysterious about the principle of order that we see illustrated in this sequence except that, whereas the artists of earlier cen-

red   blue

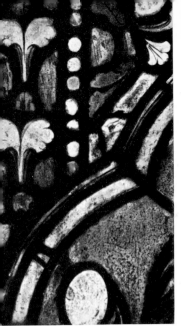

71   72   73   74

71. Ornamental Detail, French, 13th century.

72., 73. and 74. Canterbury.

turies seemed almost to live and breathe it, we seem to have to struggle to employ it. Obviously this is the kind of rapport that Matisse was so concerned to establish between his mural and the Barnes gallery; it sounds like what Le Corbusier had in mind when he tells us that he "meticulously" drew the four horizons from his hilltop in Ronchamp: "These drawings are missing or lost, it is they which unlocked, architecturally, the echo, the visual echo in the realm of shape."[32] Now, after five hundred years of great solo achievements, the creation of increasingly autonomous masterpieces of art and architecture, we are trying to grasp relations between things that were then simply in the air. Even when St. Bernard wrote his famous diatribe against fantastic sculpture in the 12th century he could not help expressing himself in the style of the art: "... in the cloisters, under the eyes of the brethren engaged in reading, what business has there that ridiculous monstrosity, that amazing misshapen shapeliness and shapely mis-shapenness?" And he goes on to describe with great force and precision how "here you behold several bodies beneath one head; there again several heads upon one body. Here you see a quadruped with the tail of a serpent; there a fish with the head of a quadruped. There an animal suggests a horse in front and half a goat behind; here a horned beast exhibits the rear part of a horse." As Panofsky says, "the one phrase *deformis formositas ac formosa deformitas* tells us more about the spirit of Romanesque sculpture than many pages of stylistic analysis."[33]

However much stained glass is an art of painting, it must be conceived primarily as an art of the wall, an art of *fenestration*. From an architectural point of view its resources are the gamut of variations between the solid wall at one extreme and the open space at the other. It may express anything from the raucous punctuation of the massive wall in Ronchamp to the shimmering membrane in Maria Königin – the solid dematerialized or the void embodied.

90

75   76   77

75., 76. and 77. Chartres.

Nothing more need be said about the luminosity of stained glass except perhaps that, since transmitted light gives to even the deepest, most saturated colors an unparalleled brilliance, one often finds one's self working less for a sufficient richness of color than for an effective degree of sobriety. Hence the wisdom of the best medieval glass painters, who seldom worked with more than eight or nine colors and often with less. In addition to the "texture of light" discussed in Chapter I, there is a continuous scale of physical textures, the texture of glass-to-lead or glass-to-concrete, the texture of panel-to-armature within a single window, and the texture of window-to-window within the wall.

Obviously, the relation between stained glass and architecture is not the same as that between sculpture or mosaic or any other medium and architecture. In fact, each medium offers such a unique range of possibilities and is bound by such a unique set of limitations that from a strictly technical point of view there is no such thing as *the* relation between art and architecture. What all such relations have in common, however – and ehre lies the rub – is that all of them, beyond the simplest treatment of art as a kind of very elegant but transitory furnishing, pose a problem of meaning or focusing of significance within an ensemble of elements. The minute art becomes an integral part of a building, it enters a hierarchy of forms, it becomes like all other visible parts a greater or lesser member of the whole. Ornament, as Sir Kenneth Clark says, "is inseparable from hierarchy. It is not only the result, but the cause of status. The carving on the corner capitals of the Doge's Palace and the central window of the Palazzo Farnese confer a kind of kingship on these points of the buildings. In a democratic building, where all windows are equal, no ornament is permissible; although I understand that the higher executives may have more windows."[34]

Page 92: 78. Ludwig Schaffrath: Baptistery Window, St. Walburga, Overath, 1954.

Page 93: 79. M. Prachensky: Catholic Parish Church, Ruhstorf; Hans Schädel, Architect.

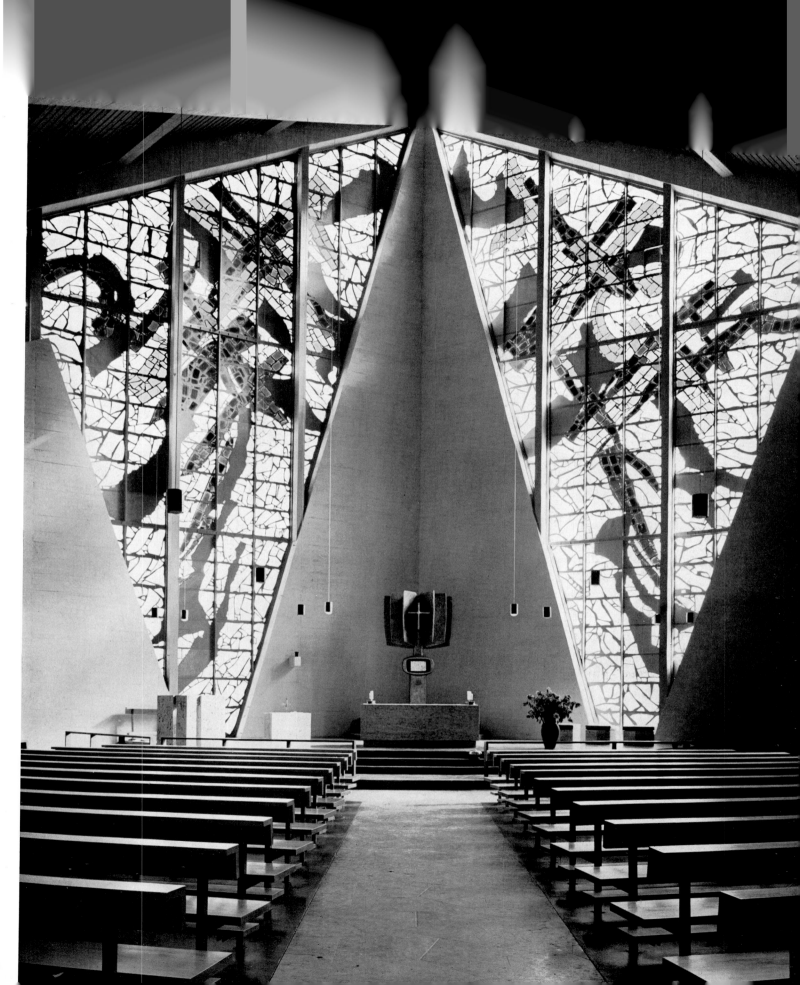

To what extent in any given instance should art *simply* ornament architecture, and to what extent should architecture set off the artist's *image*? The question really has no single, simple answer. Though architects may claim priority for their medium since it is architecture that must establish the larger context, it is no less true that when the image is sufficiently important, it becomes the function of architecture to serve that image. Thus one finds Michelangelo – whom no one can accuse of having had a painter's bias – actually destroying the Renaissance symmetry of the Sistine Chapel, removing the windows and moldings of the end wall in order to create a giant canvas for his *Last Judgment*. The way that art is related to architecture in any given case *is itself a part of the aesthetic statement*, and as variable as the resources of the particular medium make it. Stained glass, for example, may be quite validly treated at one extreme as little more than the colored infilling in a structure that itself says nearly everything that wants to be said; at the other extreme it may play a highly important iconic role, a role as important as that played by the mosaic *Pantocrators* in the Byzantine churches; the entire wall of a building may be made of stained glass and yet be treated very decoratively, as in Maria Königin, or the smallest windows may be conceived as very concentrated images. Whatever the relation established, it, the art, and the architecture may *each* vary tremendously in quality or effectiveness in any given instance. Rarely is any complex creation, whether it be a novel, a symphony or an architectural ensemble, of equal quality throughout. Thus, for example, the stained glass in Ronchamp is incredibly crude both in design and workmanship, yet it is absolutely right in spirit for Ronchamp; while the Church of Maria Königin, a most self-effacing structure, achieves with its stained-glass walls qualities of which in Ronchamp there is no hint. One is grateful to these two great creations not alone for themselves but finally also for the tremendous scope of possibilities that they imply – for demonstrating that, as Rudolf Arnheim very correctly insists, "what aspects of the world are to be made visible is a matter of philosophical creed."[35]

80. Le Corbusier: Stained-glass Window, Ronchamp.

IX COLLABORATION

When should the artist be brought into an architectural project? Doubtless, one could compile a whole dreary casebook of instances when, as Sybil Moholy-Nagy once put it, the artist had been approached at the last minute "to fig-leaf an aesthetic blunder or curry cultural prestige." And yet in any number of other instances – take only the Barcelona Pavilion and the Barnes Foundation mural – there was actually no collaboration between the architect and the artist at all. In the one case the architect and in the other the artist accepted as final and valid what the other one had already independently created and was not in the least handicapped by this aesthetically. Let us review the possible alternatives: at one extreme the artist may, like Matisse at Vence, more or less be his own architect; or the artist may be called in at the very beginning of a project, just as the structural engineer or anyone else with special knowledge is called in. He is after all an expert in his field, or should be – the stained-glass artist is among other things a kind of lighting engineer. Or the architect may completely design his building and then commission art for it; or actually build his building and then find art for it; or finally he may be, like Le Corbusier, his own artist. Which way is best? The question is obviously academic.

Actually, a strong case can be made *against* bringing the artist into a project too soon. For if, as Louis Kahn maintains, "the space should talk to the painter," then "the collaboration between the painter . . . and the architect is not necessary from the start. In fact it might be very detrimental because he is working in the realm where painting is . . . a good architect . . . will *sense* painting, he will *sense* sculpture, he will sense all those things, and he won't have to have the painter tell him that this is a good space for a painting. In fact, if he doesn't know it, it is just as well. If only he makes his spaces wonderful, so that the painter enters in and only hopes for the opportunity to make it greater than it is. This is the painter's role. Even what he will paint will change. His whole role as a painter will change, if only the architecture becomes something that one can talk about instead of just photograph . . ."[36]

However, it is not invariably true, as the latter part of Kahn's statement seems to imply, that if the architecture is simply good enough it will automatically define a role for the artist. For as Dean Burchard has observed, many fine buildings "have excluded the artists by the nature of their own designs"[37] – Kahn's among them – while certain lesser buildings like the church in Audincourt, for example, have incorporated art most effectively. Few artists or architects seem willing to accept the fact that for art and architecture to become a convincing unity *each must in some way demand the other for its own completion*. The Barcelona Pavilion needed its statue as much as Chartres needs its portals. What this unwillingness betrays is the anxious inability of both artists and architects, by and large, to visualize anything but totally self-determined, completely autonomous creations. How far we have fallen from the innocent confidence even of the ancient Greeks: when Praxiteles was asked which of his own marbles he preferred, he answered, "Those that Nicias colored!"

Is it true that a building nowadays must be totally and absolutely the creation of the architect in order to be great? Rudolf Schwarz's St. Anna Church in Düren, in which artists and artisans were most felicitously employed in half a dozen ways, teaches us that this is not necessarily so. Must the work of art always be completely autonomous in order to be worthy of the name? Audincourt, Vence and Les Bréseux tell us that they need not be. Are such works as these mere anachronisms, going somehow against the grain of the times? How then do we account for the fact that the performing arts, in which collaborative efforts are absolutely essential, have not died out altogether? Or that in jazz, that most modern of the arts, the best men seem able almost at will to function as composers, performers, accompanists and arrangers – to command the whole gamut of relations, major and minor, to a central idea?

If the creative process were absolutely orderly, like the development of forms in a growing organism, all the parts of an architectural ensemble would evolve simultaneously, with each part at each step mutually determining and being determined by all the others. In fact, the most that the architect or any other creator can consciously do – and the least that he can conscientiously do – is to keep clarifying the role that each element is to play as his work evolves, so that none ever has a chance to become too tenuous and problematical, its form hopelessly alienated from the rest. It is finally a matter for the architect to know when, in the given instance, the artist *must* be consulted: when decisions about a particular mural or sculptural conception must be made *that clearly go beyond his own special competence*. And it is a measure of his own artistic integrity to be able to recognize that moment. To quote Mr. Kahn again, "You feel the need for a piece of sculpture. The architect feels it of course. The sculptor does not know about this job, you see, so therefore it would do both of them well to call in the sculptor at that point and say ... 'Do you feel I need something here?' He might say, 'I don't know, I really can't tell. I have not seen a building like this.' Whatever it happens to be. Or he says, 'I don't know, I'm not sure. Build the building and we'll find out if you need it there.' Or he might say, 'Yes! Absolutely! It needs to be there.' It has to be some kind of relationship like that ... both have to be artists to begin with, really dedicated to their work ..."[38]

82. The St. Anna Shrine, St. Anna, Düren; Rudolf Schwarz, Architect, 1954.

83. Ewald Mataré: The Altar Cross, St. Anna.

84. Günther Haese: "Mother with Children," North Wall, St. Anna.

Right: 85. "Tree of Life," East Wall, St. Anna.

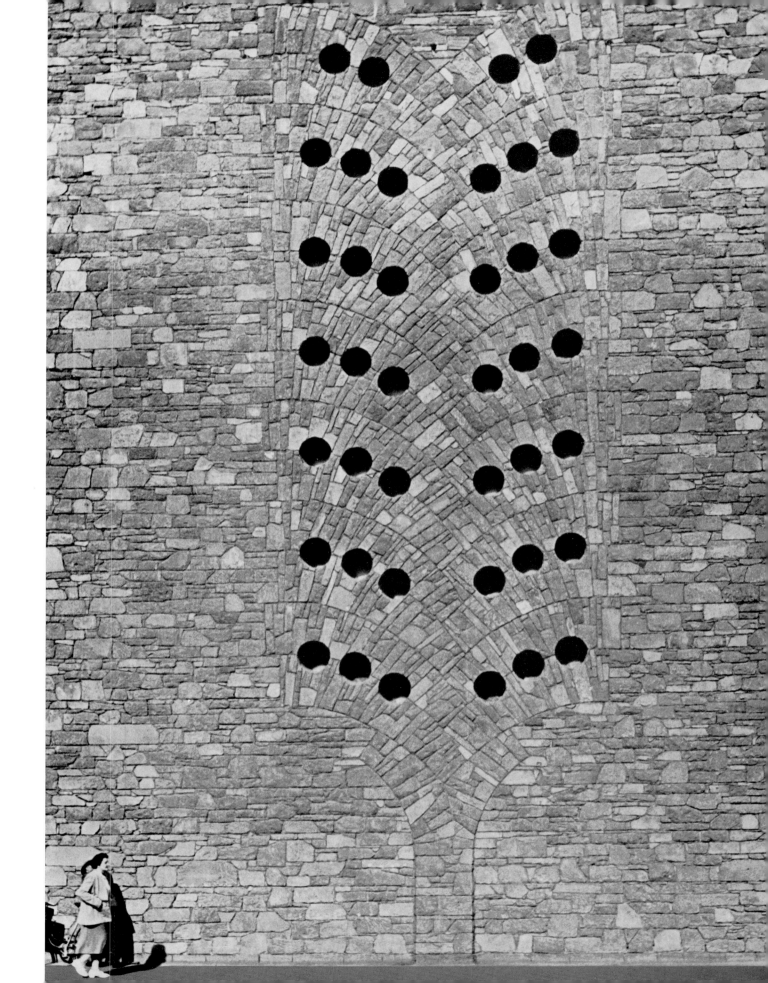

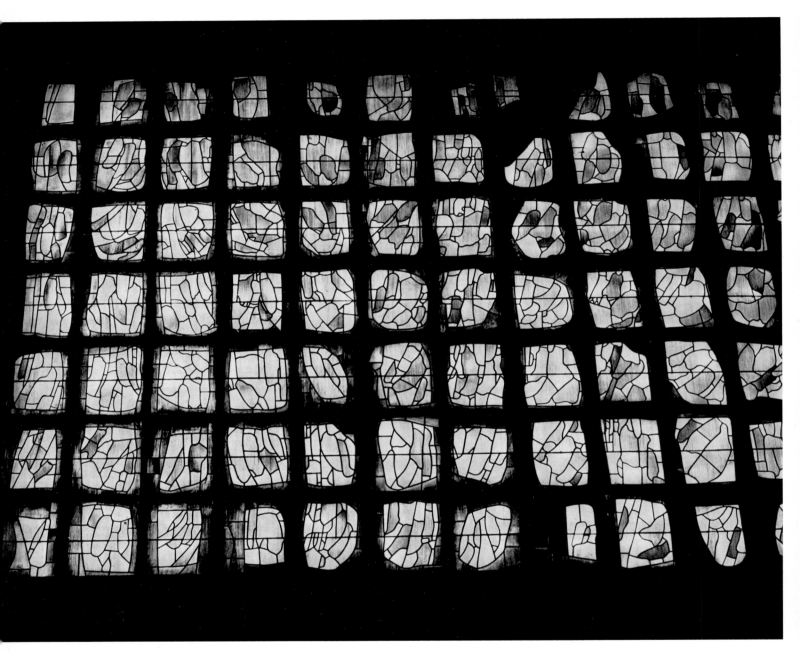

86. Jean Weinbaum: Escheranbe (Moselle); Paul Aynés, Architect.

Right: 87. First Presbyterian Church, Stamford, Connecticut; Wallace K. Harrison, Architect.

89. Leon Zack: Notre-Dame-des-Pauvres, Issy-les Moulineaux; H. Duverdier and J.-B. Lombard, Architects, 1955.

Left: 88. St. Anthony's Church, Essen; Rudolf Schwarz, Architect.

90. and 91. Johannes Schreiter: West Window, Catholic Parish Church, Bürgstadt; Hans Schädel, Architect.

Right: 92. Gabriel Loire: Trinity Church, Mannheim; Helmut Striffler, Architect.

93. Robert Pinart: Temple Emanuel, Denver, Colorado; Percival Goodman, Architect.

94. and 95. Kimie Bando: Chapel of Saint-Rouin, Argonne;
R. P. Raysiguier, Architect, 1959.

97. Walther Benner (center) and Anton Wendling (side windows): Choir, Aachen, 1951.

Left: 96. Georg Meistermann: St. Wendel's Church, Frankfurt-am-Main; Johannes Krahn, Architect, 1957. *Photograph: Das Münster.*

98. Claude Idoux, Albert Lenormand, Denise Chesnay, and Paul Reynard, upper windows; François Stahly and Etienne Martin, sculptured aisle windows: St. Remy, Baccarat; Nicolas Kazis, Architect.

99. and 100. Harry MacLean: St. Ludwig's Evangelical Church, Freiburg im Breisgau; Horst Linde, Architect.

101. Samuel Wiener, Jr.: Temple Beth El, Rochester, New York; Percival Goodman, Architect.

Right: 102. and 103. Helmut Landir: Christ Church, Bochum; Dieter Oesterlen, Architect.

Page 114: 104. Pierre Chevalley: Baptistery, Nîmes; Maurice Novarina, Architect.

PART THREE: THEMES AND VARIATIONS

"When you begin to paint on panels in the name of the Holy Trinity, always invoking that name and that of the glorious Virgin Mary, begin first of all with the foundations of glue in their different kinds."

Cennino Cennini

X THE PROBLEM OF SUBJECT MATTER

Nothing is so vital to the artist as the "subject" that his vision wants to evoke, illumine and configure. Try to imagine Matisse painting a *Guernica*, or Monet a *Crucifixion*, or Goya a view of Hampstead Heath; ask yourself what Chardin would have seen in Guardi's Venice, or Fra Angelico in the battle of San Romano; realize how different were the worlds evoked in the scriptoria of León and Winchester a thousand years ago and you must wonder how the artist is ever able to do justice to an established theme.

For the stained-glass artist this question is anything but academic; in fact, for him it is almost inescapable since a large part of his work is commissioned by churches. And yet the question is seldom thoroughly aired. It is easy to see why. For the plain fact is that a considerable body of religious art has been created in our time, some of it by our most esteemed painters and sculptors, that is neither very religious nor very good art. Must we conclude from this that religious art is a contemporary impossibility? Meyer Schapiro has declared that "the creation of medieval art did not require deeply religious artists but rather artists who had been formed within a stable religious milieu, and whose craft had been developed in tasks set by the Church .·. Hegel said very justly that in an age of piety one does not have to be religious in order to create a truly religious work of art, whereas today the most deeply pious artist is incapable of producing it."[39]

Here again, as in the problems of collaboration and the integration of the arts, I find the evidence less confining than the generalization. Here again there are, on the one hand, the powerful exceptions to the rule: Ronchamp, St. Anna in Düren, and Louis Kahn's projected Mikveh Israel Synagogue in Philadelphia; certain paintings by Rouault and Chagall, and sculpture by Barlach come immediately to mind. On the other hand, the more one studies the religious milieux of earlier times the more one wonders how stable they actually were, especially in the minds of those living then?

The Sistine ceiling, for example, is one of the very greatest monuments in all of Christian art, and yet we know that Michelangelo did everything he could to get out of having to paint it. He thought of himself as a sculptor rather than a painter, he had done no frescoes since his apprenticeship days, and he knew that the ceiling would be a back-breaking labor. Shortly after the commission was first broached, Michelangelo abruptly

Left: 105. Fragment of a 15th-century window, Madley, England.

left Rome, in fear of physical danger and in a rage of disgust with his impetuous patron, Pope Julius. During this period of self-imposed exile he wrote a sonnet that begins with the lines:

> Here helms and swords are made of chalices:
> The blood of Christ is sold so much the quart:
> His cross and thorns are spears and shields; and short
> Must be the time ere even His patience cease . . .

It is signed "Vostro Michelagnolio, in Turchia," an ironic reference to the fact that the artist was at one point even considering the possibility of going to work for the Sultan.[40]

Two centuries earlier we find Dante, in 1302, sentenced to death by fire, forced to flee from his native Florence and revenging himself by inflicting eternal torments upon his enemies in the *Divine Comedy*.

Shortly before this we find the archbishops of Paris and Canterbury formally condemning the writings of Thomas Aquinas for their heretical materialism after his death in 1274 and, as Prof. Herbert J. Muller reminds us, "it took his Dominican order fifty years of politics to get him canonized."[41]

If we go back farther still, to the celebrated moment in the mid-12th century when the rich and noble bound themselves like oxen to the carts hauling provisions to the cathedral sites of northern France, we are surely at the religious highpoint of the Middle Ages: "while they draw the waggons, we may see this miracle that, although sometimes a thousand men and women, or even more, are bound in the traces (so vast indeed is the mass, so great is the engine, and so heavy the load laid upon it), yet they go forward in such silence that no voice, no murmer, is heard . . ."[42]

Can we read in the surviving Royal Portal and tower of Chartres, built during this period, some impress of this great ground-swell of religious feeling? That they are superb creations it goes without saying, but do we find expressed in them any religious quality, any infusion of communal energy that is not also evident in, say, the sculpture at Autun? The *Christ in Glory* at Chartres may be directly compared with the Christ in the *Last Judgment* at Autun, and the latter is certainly the more compelling of the two. It is the work of one man, the far from anonymous Giselbertus who affixed his name to the tympanum and carved much of the other sculpture in the church as well. Giselbertus worked at Autun for some ten years it has been recently established,[43] from 1125 to 1135, or roughly twenty years before the great religious revival described by Abbot Haymo. But in the same account from which we have already quoted, the Abbot begins by describing the religious *decay* of his own, and presumably Giselbertus's, generation: it "had almost forgotten God," he tells us. "If it had not been for this revival, Christ would have found no faith and no faithful people left on earth . . . All had wandered away from God: all had become abominable in their iniquities."

106. Christ of the Tympanum, West Portal, Chartres, c.1150.   107. Christ of the Tympanum, West Portal, Autun, c. 1132.

Also, as Prof. Coulton observes, the Abbot's letter makes it perfectly clear that this great moment of popular dedication "was as sudden in its passing-away as in its rise. He says in so many words, concerning the dragging of the chariots to the Cathedral of Chartres: 'He who hath not seen these things will never see their like again.' Yet in 1145 we are only at the beginning of the great era of cathedral-building; this same popular effort which Haymo describes at Chartres would have been welcome all through France, not only during all Haymo's lifetime but far beyond."[44]

Each moment in history doubtless favors certain kinds of creation – presents its artists with singular opportunities and applauds achievements of a distinctive kind; but it does not on that account preclude or invalidate the scepticism of an Abelard in the 12th century, the visions of a Blake in the 18th century, or the pure joy of a Matisse in our own century. As Jacques Barzun wrote in another context, "the error has consisted in supposing that what unites an age are common opinions and common traits. If this were true what would become of the war of opinions which characterizes every age? If it were true, how could John Dewey and T. S. Eliot belong to one and the same culture? If it were true, how could there be any traditions handed down through time? There would be, on the contrary, blocks of unanimous people holding the stage for a century or so, followed by other solid blocks of an opposite complexion."[45]

The picture I have drawn is of course a one-sided one, but no more so than the far more prevalent tendency to attribute everything to the "spirit of an age" and nothing to the frequently contrary tenor of some of its very best minds, nothing to the inner momentum of art nor to the crucial importance sometimes even of single works. As Sir Kenneth Clark has observed, "The points of dogma for which no satisfactory image can be created tend to be dropped from popular religious exposition, and episodes which have scarcely occupied the attention of theologians tend to grow in importance if they produce a compelling image ... Let me give an example of iconographic triumph and disaster from one painter in one place: Titian in Venice. In the Frari his sublime image of the Assumption of the Virgin is so corporeally convincing that it provided a point of departure for Baroque painting, and this image was to float in the background of Catholic imagination down to our own day. In the 'Salute' is Titian's painting of the Pentecost, a work over which he took great pains, but without success. It was the final blow to a subject which had never found an impressive iconographical form, and which in spite of its theological importance, gradually faded from the consciousness of popular Catholicism."[46]

Though medieval art was developed to a large extent in tasks set by the Church (although by no means exclusively – let us not forget the amount of art and craft that was devoted to fortifications and armament, to the image and trappings of chivalry) and thus pervasively formed by the Church in a general way, we must not forget even there the dialogue that always takes place between men – between the artist and his patron on the one hand and between them both and the work that is created on the other hand. No work of art worthy of the name can ever be totally preconceived, no one ever quite knows what its effect will be until people have been affected by it. Once the new choir in St. Denis was completed, Abbot Suger could no longer live with his Carolingian nave, and under most of the great churches there is a regular palimpsest of foundations increasing the original one in all its dimensions. The history of medieval art is a history of continuous evolution not only of techniques but of formal and even thematic experimentation, almost from the very start.

The first Roman churches are for the most part basilican in form – old St. Peter's, Sta. Maria Maggiore, S. Clemente; then, circa 475 A. D., we get S. Stefano Rotondo, circular in plan; San Vitale in Ravenna, completed in 547, is octagonal; Aix-la-Chapelle, 796–804, is sixteen-sided. In the 7th century the Roman Pantheon was converted from a pagan temple into a church without any significant architectural changes – and later Haghia Sophia was as readily converted into a mosque by the Turks; in the very springtime of cathedral building the Abbot Suger and St. Bernard were at opposite poles on the question of whether the House of God ought to be as splendid, or as austere, as man could possibly make it; and though the Cistercians laid down a very specific plan for the church, it was soon cast aside, utterly superseded by the Gothic form, just as the

Gothic was in due course to give way to the classic, the Mannerist and the Baroque.

If we turn from architecture to imagery, we find that so central a subject as the *Crucifixion* cannot be traced back any farther than the 5th or 6th century; the Christ of the 5th century is typically blond and beard-less, a very youthful Good Shepherd. By the 12th century he is the swarthy and bearded *Pantocrator* of Byzantium throughout most of Europe; then, in the 15th and 16th centuries, he becomes blond again in northern Europe; in Quattrocento Florence, however, he is extremely fair in the paintings of Fra Angelico, considerably darker in those of Masaccio and Piero della Francesca. If we test the well-known convention that the Virgin's robe shall be blue, we find that in fact, as Prof. Coulton demonstrates, "until about A. D. 1300, it is actually the exception for her to appear in a blue cloak, or with any conspicuous blue in her garments. By 1400, it has become still more exceptional to find her without that blue mantle . . ." Before 1300, she was "royally arrayed; red and green, side by side with gold, were the two most aristocratic colours for dress in the Middle Ages . . . Yet later medieval moralists were never weary of rebuking the ordinary girls' love of finery by reminding them that the Blessed Virgin had been noted for the plainness of her dress."[47]

In about the year 1130, Coulton also tells us, Honorius of Autun wrote that in the Last Judgment the saved shall rise naked: "The salvation of the blessed, and their gladness, shall be their vesture . . ." But, as Coulton says, "the new cathedral at Autun was dedicated in 1132; and there, on the great west portal, is one of the earliest surviving Dooms. If medieval sculpture was so definitely dictated by Church authorities as we are often told, then it would be strange to find the theologian and the artist at variance on so important a point; remarkable, even if the one were writing in Southern Germany and the other working in Central France, and still stranger if the theologian was really none other than the local *scholasticus*, the master of the cathedral theological school. For, in fact, all the blessed are clothed at Autun; it is only the damned who are cast down to hell in their naked deformity."[48]

To say then that medieval imagery "was never left to individual fancy but was a very strictly ordered science, is almost the direct opposite of the truth." Coulton concludes: "Aquinas accepted the popular eschatology, and wove it into his philosophical system with marvellous labour and skill. An equally great mind might, by the devotion of a life-time, have welded popular ideas of artistic symbolism into an equally harmonious and durable whole; but the game was evidently not worth the candle. There never existed, therefore, a complete and authoritative system of symbolism in medieval art. Some of the most important points were left to individual choice, others were interpreted differently by different writers, or by the same writer. Emile Male's valuable volumes show how much was systematized; yet it is equally important, at the present time, to show how much was left unsystematized, and how little of the system

108

109

110

111

(so far as that word can be strictly used) was imposed by the hierarchy from above."[49] Written in 1928, these words are no less timely now.

Little in the way that the greatest works of Christian art actually seem to have been created justifies the belief in a once all-inspiring religious milieu that is now totally lost; little appears to justify the belief in a legalistic relation between the artist and the churchmen then or to commend it now. No formal rules for art have ever been laid down absolutely or for long, at least since the time of the Egyptians, that have not soon stifled every breath of creative energy – not only in church art but in the court academies of Mazarin, Colbert and Le Brun, in modern totalitarian states, in the carefully denatured world of mass entertainment. There has never been any certainty that the artist's most dedicated effort would produce exactly what was originally sought from him, and the artist's obligation when he undertakes to create religious, or indeed any other kind of public *art* is no different now than it has ever been. The chief value of art for religion stems from the very fact that art can give explicit form to aspirations that the language of doctrine can only name; the chief value of religion for art is that it addresses the artist to themes that are universal, to the interpretation of very profound structures of thought which he could never have invented for himself.

In the last analysis, the artist's "subject" is simply that realm of experiences to which his particular sensibility is attuned; in the words of Malraux, "the 'subject,' whether it be a stone, the Chateau Noir, or the Passion, is that 'subject' which gives a painter the most vehement desire to paint."[50]

In this ultimate sense it may or may not encompass the specific themes of any religious doctrine, but whether it does or does not is finally a particular fact about the psyche of a particular man. The artist nowadays, who has learned to shift for himself, may often be too involved with images of his own crying for expression to lend his undivided attention to religious themes that he could very well handle; or, like Louis Sullivan, he may never be granted the opportunity to design a cathedral even though one feels that Sullivan could have done it masterfully. Or the artist may, like Renoir, create a kind of goddess for which there is no formal cult. Our stained-glass fragment from Madley is a reminder that the line between the sacred and the profane has never been clearly drawn and it is not clear now.[51] One would hardly call this fantasy Christian, yet neither is it so determinedly dispassionate as Manet's *The Dead Christ with Angels*. At least to some extent the price that "a secular age" exacts from religious art is purely statistical; it is a matter of far fewer commissions being either offered to or accepted by the right men, and thus a far slower, more fitful evolution of significant images.

There is a final aspect of the problem of the artist's "subject" that we may now consider. If we turn once more to our *Ezekiel* panel in Chapter III, we realize from the manner of its fabrication that its image is to a very large extent received. The panel itself is actually nothing more nor

Left: 108. Auguste Renoir: "The Washerwoman," (detail) (1917) bronze, 48" high, Collection, The Museum of Modern Art, A. Conger Goodyear Fund.

109. Edouard Manet: "The Dead Christ with Angels," The Metropolitan Museum of Art, Bequest of Mrs. H. O. Havemeyer, 1929. The H. O. Havemeyer Collection.

110. and 111. Two Prophets from a "Tree of Jesse" window, French, 13th century. *Victoria & Albert Museum, Crown Copyright.*

less than a consummately beautiful rendering by the glass painter of a design that was quite possibly the creation of another artist altogether. In any event, the same cartoon was clearly used with minor variations as the basis for a whole series of similar panels, now in the Victoria and Albert Museum, that originally were the borders of a *Jesse Tree* window. Such works are thus at the opposite poles from "action" paintings in which, strictly speaking, there is no *rendering* whatsoever, since the whole image is evolved in the act of painting and is never determined until the very end. A de Kooning, writes Thomas Hess, may "be turned upside down or 90 degrees at the last minute . . ."[52]

Between the extremes of such maximum preconception on the one hand and such maximum improvisation on the other one could doubtless range the methods of all the great masters in the several media from the earliest times to our own, and show how certain media or techniques within them necessarily require for purely material reasons more preconception than others – bronze casting more than wood or stone carving, tempera painting more than oil painting, oil, even now, more than watercolor. But such a study would do no more than draw our attention to the locus of each master's actual image-making activity, sometimes more and sometimes less outside the final creation itself; it would tell us nothing about the profundity of the greatest works, for "art is a conscience about form," as Dr. Coomaraswamy once defined it – at once the most obedient servant and the absolute master of everything that it touches.

NOTES

1 Eugène Viollet-le-Duc, "Vitrail," *Dictionnaire Raisonné de l'Architecture Française*, Vol. 9, 1868, published serially in English in *Stained Glass*, Vols. XXVI–XXVII, 1931–32, and in part in *Journal of the British Society of Master Glass Painters*, Vol. VII, 1937.

2 *The Lost Art: A Survey of 1000 Years of Stained Glass*, New York and London, 1954.

3 *Aesthetics and History*, New York, pp. 87–88 of the 1954 paperback edition.

4 *The Voices of Silence*, New York, 1953, p. 38.

5 London, 1960, pp. 14–15.

6 Except for the Cistercians, who in the 12th century insisted on clear glass – and with its glare achieved no doubt a kind of negative aesthetic.

7 *The Print*, New York, 1950, p. 6 of the Fifth Printing, 1961; and *Natural-Light Photography*, New York, 1952, p. 112 of the Fourth Printing, 1963.

8 *Natural-Light Photography*, ibid., p. 21: Even in black-and-white photography, according to Adams, "blue rays scatter and do not penetrate as far into the emulsion. . . as red rays. Hence photographs made with red filters always show a higher 'gamma,' or contrast, for any degree of development."

9 "Vitrail," op. cit.

10 "The Stained Glass Theories of Viollet-le-Duc," *The Art Bulletin*, Vol. XLV, No. 2, June 1963, p. 123.

11 Plausible enough that both Louis Grodecki, in his *Vitraux des Eglises de France*, Paris, 1953, and I, in *The Lost Art*, singled it out for inclusion in our analyses.

12 *English Stained Glass*, London and New York, 1926, p. vi.

13 *The Lost Art*, op. cit., p. 16.

14 *The Doors of Perception and Heaven and Hell*, New York, 1963, pp. 98–99, 105–109.

15 Erwin Panofsky, "Abbot Suger of St.-Denis," *Meaning in the Visual Arts*, New York, 1955, p. 129.

16 Since an epoxy-based concrete is now being used in the making of slab-glass windows, this technique is also sometimes now referred to as an epoxy technique. In this book the term means always transparent epoxy-on-plate glass; slab glass and concrete is always referred to as such in order to avoid confusion.

17 Sidney Tillem, "Month in Review," *ARTS*, January 1962, p. 28.

18 Cf. Winston's admirable copies of two windows in East Harling, Norfolk, reproduced in E. Liddall Armitage, *Stained Glass*, Newton, Mass., 1959, p. 58. The first of these can be compared with a color detail of the actual window in the Baker and Lammer *English Stained Glass*, op. cit., p. 157. It is a fair assumption that the obvious Victorianisms in the diagram at the beginning of this chapter are not Winston's but those of his engraver.

19 Oxford, 1847. Our excerpts are from pp. 247, 249, and 250 respectively.

20 London.

21 *Memoirs*, in a letter to Mr. Charles Wilson, dated August 18, 1857, p. 38.

22 This is a perfect description of one of the Victorian Revival windows in the choir of Canterbury.

23 Op. cit., in a letter to Mr. Wilson dated November 8, 1857, pp. 44–46.

24 Ibid., lecture, "On a Revived Manufacture of Coloured Glass used in Ancient Windows," p. 180.

25 Ibid., lecture, "The Painted Glass in Lincoln Cathedral and Southwell Minster: with some general Remarks on Glass Painting," pp. 90–91.

26 "Art in Architecture 1959," *Craft Horizons*, Jan.–Feb. 1959, pp. 10–11. The italics are Mrs. Huxtable's.

27 *The Master Builders*, New York, 1961, p. 198.
28 *Matisse, His Art and His Public*, New York, 1951, p. 241.
29 Ibid., pp. 241–42. Matisse's reference to the painting as a fresco was evidently figurative, for it was executed in oil on canvas.
30 Ibid., pp. 243–44.
31 *The Master Builders*, op. cit., p. 399.
32 *The Chapel at Ronchamp*, New York, 1957, p. 89.
33 Panofsky, "Abbot Suger," op. cit., pp. 132–33.
34 "Art and Society," *Harper's*, August 1961, p. 75.
35 "The Form We Seek," *Research in the Crafts*, New York, 1961, p. 9.
36 Louis I. Kahn, *Conference on the Integration of Architecture and the Allied Arts*, Cooper Union, November 25, 1958.
37 John E. Burchard, "Alienated Affections in the Arts," *Daedalus*, Winter 1960, p. 57.
38 Kahn, op. cit.
39 "On the Aesthetic Attitude in Romanesque Art," *Art and Thought: Essays in Honor of Dr. Ananda K. Coomaraswamy*, K. Baratha Iyer, ed., London, 1947, p. 131. Later in the same essay, on p. 148, Schapiro concludes: "Reading these (Romanesque) texts, we sense that we are in a European world that begins to resemble our own in the attitude to art and artists. There is rapture, discrimination, collection: the adoration of the masterpiece and recognition of the great artist personality; the habitual judgment of works without reference to meaning or to use; the acceptance of the beautiful as a field with special laws, values and even morality."

In this second statement it is asserted that the 12th-century conception of art is already much like our own; in the first that our own cannot possibly be like that of the Middle Ages. The only explanation proffered for the disparity, a sentence about the inappropriateness of Van Gogh's technique for religious subjects, is surely inadequate. Schapiro's essay has an instructive sequel:

Even though it was written before the post-war program of European church building had really begun, he permitted the first of these statements to be quoted by William S. Rubin as a valid conclusion in a doctoral dissertation written under Schapiro's supervision in 1956–58, and published by the Columbia University press in 1960: *Modern Sacred Art and the Church of Assy.* Rubin's book concludes with the liberal French Dominican sponsors of the Sacred Art Movement reeling, late in 1955, under the impact of an encyclical in which Pius XII condemned the participation of non-Christian artists in the decoration of churches, altogether ignoring La Tourette, the convent which the Dominicans commissioned Le Corbusier to build in 1957, and which was completed in 1960, even though Rubin amended his text in a note on p. 62 to take account of another, less favorable, event that took place as late as September 1959.

The last lines of his book follow, interspersed with my comments: "Far from being the beginning of a 'Renaissance' of sacred art, the church of Assy now seems destined to go down in history as an anomaly – in company with the equally unique chapel of Matisse and the church of Le Corbusier." Such extremes as "Renaissances" and "anomalies" by no means exhaust the spectrum of possibilities; and how valid is it to make generalizations about the state of religious art in general on the basis of the French experience with the Catholic hierarchy alone? Nowhere in Rubin's book is there any acknowledgement of the vigorous program of contemporary religious art and architecture in post-war Germany, actively supported by such leading German churchmen as the archbishops of Cologne and Freiburg, and which already by 1959–60, had resulted in a considerable body of work far more successful at its best both liturgically and aesthetically than Assy; nowhere is there any mention of the very profound respect for contemporary art evinced by such leading Protestant theologians as Dr. Paul Tillich; nowhere is there any reference to the art and architecture of recent American synagogues – and yet this conclusion is cast in a completely general form.

"Modern churches will be built, and occasionally a great modern painter will decorate one of them, but reunions of masters, such as the church of Assy witnessed, will probably never take place again." Are such "reunions" either necessary or even desirable? This all-star approach produced no more successful results in the Unesco headquarters in Paris – in a building dedicated to art itself – than it did at Assy. The best German churches, on the contrary, have been built by an architect working generally with a single artist and perhaps a number of craftsmen, as Rudolf Schwarz for example did at St. Anna in Düren (pp. 98-99); and I suspect that anyone with a professional knowledge of medieval art could point to any number of churches where, as in Autun, a major cycle of decoration was evidently entrusted to *one man*.

"An undertaking of comparably great scale and meaning must wait upon the time when established religions recreate themselves as spiritual leaders of the artistic and intellectual world or are replaced by a new idealistic synthesis having the power to inspire men of vision." Unless "comparably great scale and meaning" be taken solely to mean an equal number of famous painters and sculptors working on the same project, the first part of the statement was already false with respect to Germany by 1956, when Rubin started on his dissertation. Nor is there as a matter of historical record any such simple correlation between the quality of religious art and the quality of religious dedication as is implied in the second part. In the words of Aldous Huxley, "Religious art is sometimes excellent, sometimes atrocious; and the excellence is not necessarily associated with fervor nor the atrocity with lukewarmness . . . there is good reason to believe that, during the Counter Reformation, Catholicism was taken more seriously than at any time since the fourteenth century. But the bad Catholicism of the High Renaissance produced superb religious art; the good Catholicism of the later sixteenth and seventeenth centuries produced a great deal of rather bad religious art . . . creators of religious art are sometimes, like Fra Angelico, extremely devout, sometimes no more than conventionally orthodox, sometimes (like Perugino, the supreme exponent of pietism in art) active and open disbelievers . . . " "Faith, Taste, and History," *On Art and Artists,* Morris Philipson, ed., New York, 1960, p. 41. And finally, if "men of vision" wait to be inspired by new idealistic syntheses, who creates them?

Mr. Rubin has marred an otherwise valuable study with conclusions which all too facilely dump the whole matter back in the laps of the churches.

40 Cf. J. A. Symonds, *The Life of Michelangelo,* New York, no date, pp. 111 f. The sonnet from which I quote appears in its entirety on p. 116.

41 *The Uses of the Past,* New York, 1952, p. 254.

42 From a contemporary account by Haymo, Abbot of St.-Pierre-sur-Dives, as quoted by G. G. Coulton, *Art and the Reformation,* Oxford, 1928, p. 339. Coulton's study of the surviving documents of the Middle Ages seems awesomely comprehensive, and no one's generalizations about the period are safe who has not read him. This book was reprinted in two paperback volumes in 1958, the first entitled *Medieval Faith and Symbolism,* and the second, *The Fate of Medieval Art.*

43 Cf. Denis Grivot and George Zarnecki, *Giselbertus, Sculptor of Autun,* New York, 1961.

44 Coulton, op. cit., pp. 339 and 342.

45 *Classic, Romantic and Modern,* New York, 1961, p. 14.

46 "Art and Society," op. cit., pp. 76–77.

47 Coulton, op. cit., pp. 264–65.

48 Ibid., pp. 256–57.

49 Ibid., pp. 250–51.

50 *The Voices of Silence,* op. cit., p. 353.

51 "*Multi sunt intra qui extra sunt, et multi sunt extra qui intra sunt.*" Many are outside who believe themselves to be within, and many are within who believe themselves to be outside. St. Augustine.

52 *Willem de Kooning,* New York, 1959, p. 27.

PHOTOGRAPHIC CREDITS AND ACKNOWLEDGEMENTS

Courtesy of the artists: 14, 29, 30, 49, 51, 57, 59, 65, 86, 101, 104 – E. Liddall Armitage: 12 – George Barrows: 23 – Berko Studio: 93 – Ferdinand Bosch: 16 – Ann Bredol-Lepper: 55, 56, 62 – Pierre Joly-Vera Cardot: 94, 95 – F. H. Crossley: 5 – Otto Feil: 99 – Fisk-Moore: 34 – French Government Tourist Office: 2, 7, 76, 81 – Gasparini: 66 – Yves Guillemaut: 104 – H. Heidersberger: 103 – Hermann Hellrung: 82, 83, 84, 85 – Lucien Hervé: 26 – KLM Royal Dutch Airlines: 13 – Alfred Lammer: 33, 35 – Maquette Epi: 57 – Franz Mayer & Co.: 45 – Bernhard Moosbrugger: 20 – Dr. H. Oidtmann: 27, 44, 52, 55, 56, 62, 78, 97 – Papillon, Centre du Verre de Boussois: 40 – Artur Pfau: 88 – Robert Studio: 1 – André Sauret, Editions du Livre: 23 – Kaija and Heikki Siren: 11 – Editions d'Art Albert Skira: 8 – G. E. Kidder Smith: 10, sectional elevation on page 22, 30, 33, 34, 44, 56, 89 – Hildegard Steinmetz: 79 – Eberhard Zwicker: 90, 91 – All photographs not otherwise credited are from the Studio of Robert Sowers.

QUOTATIONS

From Matisse: *His Art and His Public* by Alfred H. Barr, Jr., copyright 1951 by The Museum of Modern Art, New York, and reprinted with its permission. – From *Art and the Reformation* by G. G. Coulton, reprinted by permission of the Cambridge University Press, New York. – From *Heaven and Hell* in *The Doors of Perception and Heaven and Hell* by Aldous Huxley, reprinted by permission of Harper & Row, Publishers, Inc., New York.